Switzerland and the Crisis of Dormant Assets and Nazi Gold

Sharp criticism was recently focused on Switzerland for its doings during World War II and the Swiss banks' policies with respect to dormant assets belonging to victims of the Holocaust, in a process that lasted more than two years, from spring 1996 to fall 1998. Through the determined action of interested parties, the whole process evolved into a violent crisis with an international dimension. This crisis finally came to an end when an overall settlement was reached under which the foremost Swiss banks agreed to pay $1.25 billion to the Jewish organisations and Holocaust victims who had taken up legal action before the American courts. The aim of this book is to lay bare the mechanics of this crisis that so violently shook Switzerland and harmed its international image. It endeavours to show how and why organisations and governments heaped attack on Switzerland. The declared and perfectly legitimate cause of the crisis was that of seeing justice for the victims of the Holocaust. Behind that lay a hidden agenda only a closer look can bring to light.

Philippe Braillard is a professor at the Faculty of Economic and Social Sciences and at the European Institute, University of Geneva.

Switzerland and the Crisis of Dormant Assets and Nazi Gold

Philippe Braillard

Translated from the French by
Denys Crapon de Caprona and André Lötter

Routledge
Taylor & Francis Group
LONDON AND NEW YORK

First published 2000 by
Kegan Paul International

Published 2014 by Routledge
2 Park Square, Milton Park, Abingdon, Oxfordshire OX14 4RN
711 Third Avenue, New York, NY 10017

Routledge is an imprint of the Taylor and Francis Group, an informa business

ISBN 978-0-7103-0671-5 (hbk)
ISBN 978-0-415-76016-4 (pbk)

British Library Cataloguing in Publication Data
A catalogue record for this book is available from the British Library

Library of Congress Cataloging-in-Publication Data
A catalogue record for this book is available from the Library of Congress

Table of contents

Introduction 7

Tale of an exceptional crisis 11

The origins of the crisis 12

The Swiss banks and the dormant accounts crisis 13

Nazi Gold, a new dimension to the crisis 19

In search of a global settlement 26

Switzerland in the eye of the storm 33

Double standards 34

Smear campaign 42

Effects of the smear campaign 48

Why was Switzerland alone in the eye of the storm ? 50

Swiss isolation 54

The part the Swiss government played 57

Vulnerable Swiss banks 60

The Swiss financial center and bank secrecy under attack 64

The brinkmanship of the Jewish organizations 69

Organizations looking for recognition 75

Radicalism and intolerance of the World Jewish Congress 78

The illusions of the global settlement 92

The ambiguous role of the United States 97

Imperial America 97

Drifts of a boycott 100

Abuses of a pernicious system : Class action suits against Swiss banks 107

Senator D'Amato's opportunism 111

Stuart Eizenstat : An emblematic ambiguity 117

A duty of remembrance 123

Dormant assets: The lessons to learn 130

Was Swiss neutrality immoral ? 135

The difficult issue of Nazi Gold 142

The distressing problem of refugees 151

The requirements and the limits of a new reading of history 154

The crisis, a catalyst for challenging national identity 161

Challenging Swiss identity and its founding myths 162

The dangers of the Swiss exception 167

Toward openness and solidarity 169

Epilogue : Switzerland, the first stage in a global strategy 171

Introduction

The case against Switzerland seems overwhelming! Can the country ever be the same again? Switzerland the democrat, the political, economic and social haven of the world, the neutral promoter of peace and humanitarian causes...will she ever arise from the ashes?

Since spring 1996 the gravest of accusations have been leveled at Switzerland. It was said that the country had used its neutrality as a cover-up for selfish, cowardly and even criminal activities. It was accused of having sold its soul to the devil, to Hitler, becoming his zealous banker, supporting the Nazi war machine through dishonest financial transactions, and growing rich thanks to the laundering and receiving of goods stolen from the victims of the Third Reich. The country was even said to have shut its gates to tens of thousands of Jews fleeing the Holocaust, thus effectively sealing their fate. The Swiss banks also stood accused of having used, once the war was over, their famed secrecy to keep the descendants or victims of the Holocaust from recovering the money they had sought to put in a place of safety.

These serious accusations were brought by Jewish organizations, primarily the World Jewish Congress. Several political organizations also took them up. The fact that the accusations were part of a larger process by which the responsibility of the international community in the darkest hour of the century was freshly assessed, made no difference. It was Switzerland that featured in the crudest light, which stood condemned firstly and foremostly. It stood accused of the basest of compromises, and of craftily having covered up its guilt for almost half a century.

The accusers of Switzerland and the country's past did not, however, limit themselves to mere accusations. They have also claimed financial compensation – especially from the Swiss banks – for needy survivors or descendants of Holocaust victims. And with some American States and cities going as far as imposing sanctions on Switzerland and the Swiss banks, the pressure kept rising. This crisis was to last two full years. It finally came to an end when an overall settlement was reached under which the Swiss Big Three banks agreed to pay 1.25 billion dollars to the Jewish organizations and Holocaust victims who had taken up legal action before the American courts.

The aim of this book is to lay bare the mechanics of this crisis that so violently shook and harmed Switzerland's international image. It endeavors to show that it is impossible to understand this issue if one takes the protagonists' declarations and motivations at face value. It argues that only by taking a deeper look one can understand why the matter has reached such alarming proportions, why the Jewish organizations and some American politicians so doggedly heaped attack on attack on Switzerland. The declared and perfectly legitimate cause of the crisis was that of seeing justice done to the victims of the Holocaust. But behind that there was a hidden agenda only a closer look can bring to light.

But, may one ask, is it lawful at all to cast the cold look of political analysis on a process whereby justice and redress were sought for a nation that had been subjected to what was certainly the most horrendous genocide in human history? Is it lawful to take up a project such as this? Will a book like this not inevitably go beyond a kind of sacred frontier, trivializing or making people forget the horror of the unspeakable tragedy of the Holocaust? I have often asked myself this difficult, even heart-rending question while I was working on this book. Therefore, had I not come to believe that there are clear answers to these questions, I would never have been able finish it. I believe that a cold, hard look at the main protagonists in this crisis in no way whatsoever can harm the legitimate rights of the Holocaust survivors. Thc contrary is true: it is the hidden agenda, undisclosed ambitions, selfish interests and often dishonorable methods of the seemingly ardent defenders of Holocaust victims that damage their sacred rights. It is thus the sanctity of the victims' rights that justify, and even ask for a book like this.

Once the main protagonists' true face is exposed we can truly understand the crisis. Only then we realize what this really is: a masquerade, a tragic masquerade!

Chapter one

Tale of an exceptional crisis

It was in April 1996 that the dormant account crisis first started. The affair was to throw the Swiss banks, and through them the entire Swiss nation into a critical process that would last for more than two years. American newspapers were the first to publish articles on the dormant accounts of Jewish Holocaust victims allegedly kept by the Swiss banks more than fifty years after the end of the war. The press articles referred to documents and testimonies first brought to public attention by the GOP Senator from New York, Alfonse D'Amato. These documents purported that the Swiss bankers made it virtually impossible for heirs of Holocaust victims to recover assets deposited in Switzerland. Senator D'Amato further increased publicity on the issue by organizing and presiding over a hearing into the matter before the Senate Banking, Housing and Urban Affairs Committee on April 23 1996. President Clinton himself announced that he would fully support an in-depth investigation by Senator D'Amato into the matter. Several Jewish organizations then joined the fray, notably the World Jewish Congress, asking for explanations from the Swiss banks. With accusations spreading to gold transactions between Switzerland and Nazi Germany a few months later, the crisis was soon to take an even more serious turn.

The origins of the crisis

But it was no coincidence that the crisis, which as we saw initially centered on dormant accounts only, reached a critical point in April 1996. The process had really started several years before, now only coming to its natural and logical result. A too superficial approach to the crisis will not reveal the impulse behind it. We will therefore have to take a look at earlier developments too.

The crisis undoubtedly had its origins in the end of the Cold War. The collapse of communism in Eastern Europe and the implosion of the Soviet empire profoundly changed the geopolitical order in Europe. Suddenly there was no threat of war between NATO and the Warsaw Pact countries anymore. All over Eastern Europe democratic governments replaced communist ones. This meant that Europeans could after many decades of silence afford to cast a new look on the blackest moments of their past. Since the '40s the Cold War had made such introspection impossible. Faced with the Soviet threat, Western Europe had to stay united. It could thus ill-afford to fish for possible abuses their allied partners had committed in the Second World War.

Another element further increased the drive for truth from the beginning of the '90s, i.e. the opening up by several countries of their secret archives. This aroused the interest of many researchers. Obviously freedom of access to information is not the main reason behind the crisis since some archives were opened up in the '80s already, as was the case in Switzerland. Moreover, most of the principal facts in the dormant accounts and Nazi Gold cases were known or available as early as 1945.

But there is a world of difference between having information and using information, drawing logical conclusions from it.

The natural outflow of the new political context in Europe was that Eastern European Holocaust survivors, or the heirs of Holocaust victims use their new-found freedom to try to recover their belongings. In the same way Jewish organizations, e.g. the World Jewish Congress and the Jewish Agency, which for decades had to concentrate all their efforts on Jews living in communist countries and the troublesome emigration of some of them to Israel, could redirect their attention to helping Central and Eastern European Jews to obtain compensation for the losses they suffered during World War II. These organizations also founded the World Jewish Restitution Organization in 1993, giving it the task of recovering the assets stolen from Jews in Central and Eastern Europe during the war. To achieve this aim, it is understandable that the Jewish organizations decided to take a close look at the way Jews were treated by the countries involved in the war, including neutral European States.

The Swiss banks and the dormant accounts crisis

The search for dormant accounts belonging to nationals of Central and Eastern European countries quickly led to Switzerland. Indeed, many endangered Jews seemed to have opted to put their assets in Swiss banks. The Jewish organizations, notably the World Jewish Congress, therefore thought it fit to ask the Swiss banks to again take up the search for dormant accounts dating back to World War II. These accounts had already been the subject of several petitions made by Jewish organizations immediately after the war and during the '50s, and finally resulted in a 1962 Swiss federal decree that ordered the

Swiss banks to look for dormant assets and return them to their legitimate owners or, for lack of that, to turn them over to charity.[1] However, the Jewish organizations considered that the Swiss banks' searching had been anything but exhaustive and that there were still many Holocaust dormant accounts. We thus see that the new global context of the beginning of the '90s favored the reopening of the case.

In Switzerland itself several people, especially Members of Parliament, drew attention to dormant accounts.[2] The commemoration of the 50th anniversary of the end of World War II afforded the Swiss administration an opportunity to take a fresh look into this dark period. Switzerland indeed fully intended to reveal its own offenses. An example was the very moving speech Swiss President Kaspar Villiger delivered before Parliament on May 7, 1995. He apologized that Switzerland had let the German authorities put a "J" stamp on Jewish passports. Also, from spring of 1995 the Swiss press started to take an interest in Jewish dormant accounts and Nazi bank accounts in Switzerland. Round about the same time the Israeli press published a few articles on the issue.

The case took on a new dimension when, in June 1995, the *Wall Street Journal*[3] published an article accusing Julius Baer, a bank in Zurich, of holding dormant assets belonging to Holocaust victims and of obstructing attempts by their heirs to recover their money. This article had far-reaching effects because it coincided with a campaign launched by the World Jewish Congress on dormant assets. The aim of the Congress

---

[1] Federal decree of December 20, 1962, on assets deposited in Switzerland by foreigners or stateless persons persecuted for racial, religious or political reasons.

[2] Ordinary question by Piller on December 6, 1994; ordinary question by Ziegler on March 7, 1995; Grendelmeier parliamentary initiative of March 24, 1995; Piller motion of June 12, 1995.

[3] *Wall Street Journal*, June 18, 1995.

was that the Swiss banks change their attitude and open their archives, thereby allowing the owners of the dormant accounts to identify and recover their assets.

The accusations fell on the hearing ears of Hans Baer, then president of the bank Julius Baer. In an effort to find an equitable solution to the dormant accounts issue, Mr. Baer, along with several other members of the Swiss Bankers' Association, began talks with the World Jewish Congress as early as September 1995. Thanks to the talks the Swiss Bankers' Association reached an agreement with the World Jewish Congress and the World Jewish Restitution Organization on May 2, 1996. By that time the dormant accounts issue had reached crisis point, notably because of the persistent accusations of Senator D'Amato. Under the agreement was set up a Committee of Eminent Persons, also known as the Volcker Committee – after the name of its chairman, Paul Volcker, a former chairman of the U.S. Federal Reserve Board. The main task of the Volcker Committee was to carry out a large-scale audit of all Swiss banks, identifying all dormant accounts opened before, during and immediately after World War II.

On January 1, 1996, came into force two decisions taken by the Swiss Bankers' Association. The first created a Bank Ombudsman whose task it was to facilitate the search for dormant accounts at the plus minus 400 Swiss banks. The other decision introduced new directives on the treatment of Swiss bank accounts and deposits.

But these measures were unable to prevent the dormant accounts issue to turn into a full-blown crisis in the course of 1996. Thus hardly one month after the two decisions came into force, relations between the Swiss Bankers' Association and the Jewish organizations became severely strained when the Association announced that its internal audit had found a total of 775 dormant accounts worth 38.7 million Swiss francs.

The Jewish organizations believed this amount to be far below true figures and called the Swiss Bankers' Association search into question.

Throughout spring 1996, the American press vehemently attacked the Swiss banks, largely echoing Senator D'Amato's accusations. Then, in October 1996, the crisis took a legal turn when the Holocaust survivors and heirs of victims lodged two collective complaints (class action suits) before the American courts. October 1996 also saw the Senate Banking Committee give a second hearing on the Swiss banks and dormant accounts of Holocaust victims. The hearing, again chaired by Senator Al D'Amato, further increased tensions.

Faced with this rapidly deepening crisis, the Swiss administration was prompt to take action. The Swiss Federal Office of Foreign Affairs, fully conscious of the seriousness of the crisis and foreseeing the grave consequences it could have on Switzerland, set up a task force under Ambassador Thomas Borer on October 24, 1996. The main aim of the task force was to coordinate the activities of the different federal departments. Less than two months later the Swiss Parliament itself reacted by taking two very important decisions. The first, a federal decree passed unanimously on December 13, concerned the "historical and legal search for assets deposited in Switzerland after the rise to power of the Nazi regime". The decree made the search possible by allowing bank secrecy on related assets to be lifted for a period of five years. The second decision, taken on December 19 by the Swiss government, set up an independent commission of experts led by Swiss historian Jean-François Bergier. The Bergier Commission consisted of nine historians and lawyers from Switzerland and third countries. The commission was given the task of examining from a historical and legal point of view the scope and occurrences surrounding the assets deposited in Switzerland during the Nazi period. It also had to look into the trade in gold and foreign currency between Switzerland and Nazi Germany, the trade relations between Switzerland and the Third Reich and the Swiss policy on refugees during this period.

With such far-reaching decisions the Swiss administration hoped to once and for all settle the dormant accounts issue and bring the whole truth about Switzerland's actions during World War II to light. One could reasonably have expected that these measures would calm tensions, and even solve the crisis. But this was far from the case. Led as it were by the World Jewish Congress, the American class action plaintiffs and Jewish organizations had decided to adopt a sweeping and long-term approach. They had no incentive to reduce pressure before having obtained huge sums of money as compensation.

A few weeks later another incident further increased tensions. This was to bring the crisis to its height. In a way it was a crisis within the crisis. In an interview with a Swiss newspaper,[4] Jean-Pascal Delamuraz, who at the time assumed the rotating Swiss presidency, referred to the crisis as an attempt to destabilize Switzerland. He also described the threats of sanctions and pressure put on the Swiss banks by the Jewish organizations as "blackmail." His remarks met with the indignation of the leaders of the Jewish organizations who promptly ended all talks with Switzerland and demanded that he withdraw his remarks. The talks resumed two weeks later, but only after Mr. Delamuraz had apologized to Edgar Bronfman, chairman of the World Jewish Congress, for having hurt his and many other people's feelings.

But just as the tensions seemed to decrease, a second major incident led to yet another crisis point. Christoph Meili, an employee of a security company working for the Union Bank

---

[4] *Tribune de Genève*, December 31, 1996.

of Switzerland (UBS) in Zurich, discovered records on the Nazi period that a bank archivist was on the point of destroying. Mr. Meili saved the documents from destruction and handed them to a Jewish organization, which informed the press. In the months that followed this incident triggered a series of major events. Mr. Meili was laid off by his employer, and legal charges brought against him for breach of bank secrecy. Switzerland was to be vehemently criticized for these developments, especially for the charges against Mr. Meili. A few months later the Swiss courts dismissed the case. But the turmoil did not cease. Mr. Meili's subsequent flight to the United States on account of death threats he had been receiving was to be the focus of media attention. The U.S. warmly welcomed Mr. Meili, offering him asylum and, thanks to the intervention of Senator D'Amato, a green card. Edgar Bronfman, chairman of the World Jewish Congress, also offered him a job. In the meantime tensions between the Swiss banks and the Jewish organizations further rose on account of the refusal of the UBS to apologize for the incident. A year later Mr. Meili filed a claim for 2.56 billion dollars of damages against the bank.

On February 5, 1997, shortly after the Meili incident, Switzerland's Big Three banks decided to contribute 100 million Swiss francs to a humanitarian fund for Nazi victims. Three weeks later the Swiss government officially created the fund. Several Swiss industrial companies as well as the Swiss National Bank also contributed to the fund, raising its capital to 265 million Swiss francs. Appointment of three of the seven members on the fund's board of directors was left to the World Jewish Restitution Organization, a way to closely involve the Jewish organizations in the distribution of the funds. Rolf Bloch himself, president of the Federation of Jewish Communities in Switzerland, was to head the board. The main task of the fund was that of aiding needy victims - including their descendants -of racial, religious, political or other kinds of wartime persecution.

Exactly one month after the setting up of the fund, Swiss President Arnold Koller, in a speech delivered before the Swiss Parliament, provided details on a project to set up a foundation funded by the revaluation of the gold reserves of the Swiss National Bank to 7 billion Swiss francs. Half of the interest earned on this capital would go to foreign victims of poverty, serious human rights abuses or natural disasters. At first this plan met with a very favorable response. Especially Holocaust survivors were hoping to receive aid from the foundation. Very soon, however, enthusiasm turned into criticism. The causes for the change of mood could be found in the unclear defining of a project that had been tabled too hastily and under the pressure of the dormant accounts crisis. One of the main points at issue in both Switzerland and abroad was whether Holocaust victims would explicitly be included with the foundation's beneficiaries. The Jewish organizations (notably the Jewish Agency and the World Jewish Congress) actively participated in the debate, demanding that aid to Jewish victims of Nazism specifically feature in the charter of the foundation. Some representatives of the Jewish organizations went as far as accusing the Swiss government of creating a diversion to reduce pressure on Switzerland through this lavish but vague plan.

Nazi Gold, a new dimension to the crisis

With the publication on May 7, 1997, of a U.S. State Department report entitled "U.S. and Allied Efforts to Recover and Restore Gold and other Assets Stolen or Hidden by Germany During World War II," [5] the crisis was to take on a new dimension altogether.

The report, compiled by a group of State Department historians and overseen by Under Secretary of Commerce Stuart Eizenstat, harshly criticized Switzerland's wartime neutrality.

It addressed a wide number of issues, including the Swiss wartime refugee policy, trade relations between Switzerland and Nazi Germany and Switzerland's share of responsibility for the protraction of the war. But the main thrust of the report concerned the large amounts of gold traded between Switzerland and the Third Reich. This opened a new chapter in the crisis. The report especially faulted the Swiss National Bank's purchases of Nazi Gold from the Reichsbank because the gold had in part been looted from the central banks of occupied countries or from Holocaust victims.

The Eizenstat report, however, was not the first to mention the issue of Nazi Gold. Already in his spring '96 attacks on Switzerland, senator D'Amato mentioned gold transactions between Switzerland and Germany. And in September 1996, the British Foreign Office joined in by publishing a very critical report on the Swiss National Bank's gold purchases from Germany. But with the publication in May 1997 of the Eizenstat report, the Nazi Gold case suddenly doubled the intensity of the dormant accounts crisis. This serious development was certainly due to the harshness of the Eizenstat report, the publicity surrounding it as well as the international weight of the

---

[5] *U.S. and Allied Efforts to Recover and Restore Gold and other Assets Stolen or Hidden by Germany During World War II.* Preliminary Study Coordinated by Stuart Eizenstat, Under Secretary of Commerce for International Trade, Special Envoy of the Department of State on Property Restitution in Central and Eastern Europe. Prepared by William Z. Slany, The Historian, Department of State, Washington, May 1997.

United States. But perhaps the most conclusive factor was that the Jewish organizations took up the report's conclusions, demanding explanations from Switzerland for its gold trading with the Nazis. The Swiss administration reacted by contesting several of the report's conclusions. It also ruled out any renegotiation of the 1946 Washington Agreement, arguing that the agreement had satisfactorily settled the issue of Swiss gold purchases from Germany.

The Nazi Gold debate took a further turn for the worse the month after the publication of the Eizenstat report when the BBC broadcast, on June 18, 1997, a scathing documentary on Switzerland's wartime gold purchases from Germany. The movie, called Nazi Gold, presented Switzerland as a criminal country. Violent reactions followed, especially when it was broadcast in Switzerland a few weeks later.

But despite the turmoil over the Nazi Gold issue, the dormant accounts remained front page news throughout summer 1997. This was mainly the result of the Swiss Bankers' Association publishing in the leading Swiss and international newspapers a list of 1,756 dormant accounts of foreigners (worth 61.2 million Swiss francs) on July 23, 1997. Three months later, on October 29, 1997, the Association published a second list totaling 14,562 dormant accounts (10,875 Swiss clients; 3,687 foreign clients) worth a total of 18.8 million Swiss francs (6.17 million Swiss francs for foreign clients).

However, despite these obvious efforts of the Swiss banks at transparency, the pressure and crisis continued unabated. In fact, with the financial managers of several American States and cities threatening to boycott Switzerland, the pressure only kept rising. California and Massachusetts even decided to freeze (with immediate effect) any trade relations with Swiss banks, or at least with the Union Bank of Switzerland. In the eyes of these States the UBS grossly overstepped in the Meili case. This mistake was compounded by some UBS declarations that Holocaust survivors and Jewish organizations interpreted as insulting. On October 19, 1997, UBS president Robert Studer publicly apologized for the comments made on the dormant accounts and the Meili case. But, again, this was not sufficient to ease tensions.

October and November saw the boycott threats grow louder and more and more specific despite the fact that the U.S. administration and Mr. Eizenstat himself expressed serious doubts about boycotts. On December 8, 1997, a conference attended by some 200 representatives of state and local U.S. government agencies confirmed the boycott intentions, though suspending their application until March 31, 1998. This moratorium was intended to allow the Swiss banks to start talks with the Jewish organizations and American class action plaintiffs.

During a meeting in Zurich between representatives of the Swiss Big Three banks and Mr. Eizenstat a few days later, the banks for the first time brought up the possibility of a global settlement for the now double crisis. The idea of a global settlement was indeed rapidly gaining ground as the pressure on Switzerland by that time focused both on the dormant accounts and the Nazi Gold issues.

An example of the mounting pressure can be found in the gold conference held in London from December 2 through 4, 1997. Forty-two countries participated. For British Foreign Secretary and conference host Robin Cook, the aim was to establish the truth about the gold the Nazis had looted from the occupied countries and Holocaust victims, and to provide compensation for needy Shoah survivors. However, the president of the World Jewish Congress used to conference to launch a scathing attack on Switzerland, criticizing the country for its wartime gold trading with Germany and stating that it was still in possession of stolen gold and had to pay compensation of two to three billion dollars as a global settlement. But Swiss President Arnold Koller outright rejected any settlement running into the billions of dollars, and even qualified the request as a "provocation."[6]

Nineteen ninety eight started out with another bout of tension between Switzerland and the World Jewish Congress when Federal Councilor Flavio Cotti (then Swiss Secretary of State) remarked that foreigners had to understand Swiss disappointment and the country's rejection of the unfounded attacks from the American East Coast, especially from New York. World Jewish Congress vice-president Kalman Sultanik was outraged by these comments. For him they were tantamount to remarks made by Kurt Waldheim who at one point felt he was being victimized by East Coast pressure groups. Alan Hevesi, New York city's comptroller, and counterparts of his in four other American States were soon to endorse Mr. Sultanik's view, demanding that Mr. Cotti apologize for remarks they considered as indirect attacks on Jews. Mr. Cotti, however, was not to comply with their demands.[7]

The beginning of February again saw Senator D'Amato contributing to the tensions upon declaring that he would do everything in his power to prevent a merger between two of the Big Three Swiss banks, the Union Bank of Switzerland and the Swiss Bank Corporation. In his opinion, these banks refused to give real answers to Holocaust survivors. But with the publication by the Swiss Bankers' Association of the lists of dormant account holders a few months before still fresh in everybody's mind, Swiss public opinion saw such views as a show of con-

[6] *Neue Zürcher Zeitung*, December 13, 1997.
[7] *Tribune de Genève*, January, 3-4, 1998.

tempt and disregard for all the efforts undertaken by Switzerland to settle the dormant accounts issue.

In March the situation further worsened when the chairman of the World Jewish Congress threatened the Swiss banks with full-scale war if they refused to make a global settlement in the dormant accounts issue.[8]

By now Swiss public opinion was reeling under all the verbal abuse and threats to the country. The Swiss Jewish community itself was becoming more and more annoyed with the arrogance and aggressiveness of the World Jewish Congress and Senator D'Amato.

Yet another incident made tensions rise further between the Jewish organizations and Switzerland when, in February, two Swiss insurance companies, Winterthur and Bâloise, refused to open their archives to the U.S. administration which was now looking for dormant insurance policies of Holocaust victims. The two companies denied the U.S. access to their archives because they felt they had no obligation to comply with American laws and monitors. World Jewish Congress executive director Elan Steinberg retorted by qualifying the legal reasons of the Swiss companies as "obscene." Israel Singer, Secretary-General of the World Jewish Congress, referred to them as "scornful" and reminiscent of the Swiss banks' initial attitude in the dormant accounts issue. Senator D'Amato, who had joined the World Jewish Congress in asking that an international commission of experts be set up to search for dormant insurance policies, also harshly criticized the two Swiss insurers.

The problem of the dormant insurance policies only compounded the crisis between Switzerland and the Jewish organizations. But at least Swiss companies were not the only

---

[8] *Jewish Bulletin of Northern California*, March 1998.

ones to be targeted, unlike with the dormant accounts issue. As early as June 1997, Holocaust survivors brought a 16 billion dollars class action suit against a total of sixteen European insurance companies on account of dormant insurance policies the companies never paid out to beneficiaries. A while later the interim report of the Swiss Bergier[9] Commission further added to the companies' predicament by blaming them for their attempt – towards the end of the war – to recover debt owed them by Germany through gold transactions with the Nazi regime. Nonetheless, the dormant insurance policies were not to be included in the talks on the dormant accounts; neither were they part of the global settlement reached on August 12, 1998. A first step toward settling the insurance policy problem was taken on April 8, 1998, when four European insurance companies (Allianz, Generali, Axa and Zurich), later to be joined by Bâloise and Winterthur, signed a memorandum with the World Jewish Congress and the U.S. controllers. Finally, on September 14, 1998, they agreed to set up an international commission on dormant insurance policies.

But the insurance policy issue was not the only one to complicate matters for Switzerland at the start of 1998. On January 5, Channel 4, a British television station, broadcast a documentary accusing Switzerland of having treated 6,000 Jewish refugees from Germany like criminals, putting them in labor camps in the country. A few days later the Simon Wiesenthal Center in Los Angeles followed suit in a report taking Switzerland to task in the strongest terms possible, stating that as much as 17,000 to 22,000 refugees, for the most part Jews, had been locked away in camps in Switzerland and treated no

[9] Independent Commission of Experts Switzerland - Second World War, *Switzerland and Gold Transactions in the Second World War*. An Interim Report. Bern, June 1998.

better than slaves.[10] Switzerland strongly contested these serious accusations, stating that the Swiss internment camps could in no way be compared to German concentration camps and that no refugee had ever been a prisoner there. Soon a great number of accounts given by former Jewish refugees in Switzerland were also to belie these accusations. But the harm was done, and the climate between Switzerland and the Jewish organizations kept deteriorating.

In search of a global settlement

Tensions were also to rise in the run-up to the expiration of the moratorium on sanctions against the Swiss banks that some American States and cities had agreed on in December 1997. However, on March 26, the American and Swiss governments published a declaration asking the parties involved to let up economic sanctions. This request led to a 3-month extension of the moratorium, but only after the Big Three Swiss banks had agreed to negotiate a deal settling all the claims against them. The talks thus finally started on April 27, 1998, bringing together representatives of Switzerland's two largest banks, the World Jewish Congress, the American class action plaintiffs, and, acting as facilitator, Under Secretary of State Stuart Eizenstat.

The negotiations were to be the scene of painful haggling. The Swiss banks, and the Swiss administration itself were put under more and more pressure, notably concerning the Nazi Gold issue. The Jewish organizations and American plaintiffs wanted the Swiss National Bank to contribute to a global payout deal to Holocaust victims. They argued that the Bank had

[10] SCHOM, Alan Morris, *The Unwanted Guests: Swiss Forced Labor Camps (1940-1944)*. Los Angeles, Simon Wiesenthal Center, 1998.

conducted large-scale gold trading with Nazi Germany; and threatened, if Switzerland did not comply, to renegotiate the Washington Agreement of 1946 which had settled the problem of Swiss gold trading with Germany. Under this agreement, Switzerland had paid the Allies 250 million Swiss francs,[11] thereby contributing to the pacification and reconstruction of war-ravaged Europe.

The Swiss government, however, by the mouth of President Flavio Cotti firmly, foreclosed any possibility of the country participating financially in a global settlement. Mr. Cotti also excluded any renegociation of the Washington Agreement. Two weeks later Swiss National Bank chairman Hans Meyer, for his part also ruled out any Bank participation in a global settlement. And, as a sign of support to the Swiss government, the Federation of Jewish Communities in Switzerland even turned down an invitation to participate in the talks.[12]

But in the months that followed the Jewish organizations kept returning to the matter, notably by drawing on the interim report of the Bergier Commission on "Swiss gold trading in World War II" published on May 25, 1998.[13] According to the report the Swiss National Bank, which had bought 1.2 billion Swiss francs of gold from the Reichsbank during the war, knew as early as 1941 that Nazi Germany had included in its own gold reserves gold stolen from the central banks of the occupied countries. Even more seriously, 119.5 kg of gold stolen from Holocaust victims was beyond any doubt included in Nazi deliveries of gold to Switzerland, though it was never proven that the Swiss National Bank managers were aware of

---

[11] Present value of 1.5 billion Swiss francs.

[12] *Neue Zürcher Zeitung*, May 2, 1998.

[13] Independent Commission of Experts Switzerland - Second World War, *Switzerland and Gold Transactions in the Second World War, op. cit.*

the origin of this gold. Finally, the Bergier Commission found the Swiss National Bank's justification (e.g. neutrality, deterrence from an invasion by Germany, etc.) of gold trading with Nazi Germany unconvincing.

The Swiss government responded by deploring the lack of moral and political conviction of the wartime Swiss National Bank managers. But it also stated that the report brought out no new facts and that it was out of the question that the Swiss government meet any new demands, such as renegotiating the Washington Agreement of 1946.

The publication of the Bergier report was closely followed by the publication of the second Eizenstat report.[14] This report poured fuel to the fire of the Jewish organizations, which were now more than ever pressing the Swiss administration to contribute directly to a global payment. The Jewish organizations' reading of the second Eizenstat report was that it confirmed Switzerland's role in the supply of war equipment to Nazi Germany, especially by serving as a transit port for gold used to support the German war effort. But heightened pressure was unsuccessful in making the Swiss government go back on their firm decision not to participate in talks on a global settlement. Their own reading of the second Eizenstat report was that it was much less critical of Switzerland than the first, recognizing that Switzerland had been under a clear threat of invasion by the Axis powers.

---

[14] *U.S. and Allied Wartime and Postwar Relations and Negotiations with Argentina, Portugal, Spain, Sweden, and Turkey on Looted Gold and German External Assets and U.S. Concerns about the Fate of the Wartime Ustasha Treasury. Supplement to Preliminary Study on U.S. and Allied Efforts to Recover and Restore Gold and other Assets Stolen or Hidden by Germany during World War II.* Coordinated by Stuart Eizenstat, Under Secretary of State for Economic, Business, and Agricultural Affairs, Prepared by William Slany, The Historian, Department of State. Washington, June 1998.

These events were followed by a contradictory brouhaha in the international press on what the banks were willing to pay and what not. To make matters clearer the two biggest Swiss banks announced in a press communiqué on June 19, 1998, that they had made an offer of $600m for a global settlement, pointing out that the offer was "at the limit of what they could bear." The announcement led to violent reactions on the part of the Jewish organizations, again resulting in increased tensions between the negotiating parties. The counsels for the class action plaintiffs and World Jewish Congress described the offer as completely unacceptable. The World Jewish Restitution Organization went as far as describing it as an insult. Press leaks put the amount the counsels for the plaintiffs and World Jewish Congress were hoping to get at 1.5 billion dollars.

In an attempt to make tensions rise even higher, lawyers Michael Hausfeld and Melvyn Weiss in the name of all Holocaust victims lodged a complaint against the Swiss National Bank before the federal court of the District of Columbia on June 29, 1998. A few days later the World Jewish Restitution Organization announced that it would follow suit. The Swiss government for its part deemed the complaint "fundamentally flawed, politically unacceptable and legally unjustifiable."

But heightened pressure on Switzerland and the Swiss banks was not to bring about much change. The end of June thus saw the talks locked in stalemate. Realizing this the representatives of the States and cities, during a meeting in New York on July 1, 1998, decided to lift the moratorium on the boycott of Swiss banks. Following the meeting several American States announced that they would participate in the boycott. California thus declared that it would no longer call on Swiss banks for short-term investments, while the city and State of New York announced that they would phase in a series of sanctions against Swiss banks and companies, possibly leading to a full-scale boycott of all Swiss products in 1999. These measures led to sharp reactions in Switzerland. The Swiss Bankers' Association declared itself outraged and disappointed. The Swiss government pointed out that the sanctions were counter-productive, unjustified and illegal. Public opinion too favored a very firm reaction by the Swiss government. Talk of lodging a complaint against the United States before the World Trade Organization was rife. Some political parties in Switzerland even urged retaliatory measures.

It was at this point that Alan Hevesi, New York city's comptroller and main protagonist in the sanctions against the Swiss banks, accused the Swiss government of not living up to its promise to contribute to a global payment. Head of the Swiss task force, Ambassador Thomas Borer, sharply rejected these accusations, retorting that Mr. Hevesi was guilty of spreading false information and manipulating public opinion. He compared Mr. Hevesi's actions with intimidation tactics and propaganda. A few days later, Jewish Agency chairman Avraham Burg retorted by demanding that Ambassador Borer resign.[15]

Tensions were thus at an all-time high when the U.S. Senate Banking Committee convened the next hearing, chaired by Senator D'Amato, to examine whether there were legal grounds to reopen the 1946 Washington Agreement. Senator D'Amato, angered by the Swiss government's refusal to testify at the hearing, promptly accused Switzerland of "again ... stonewalling the truth."[16]

But despite the overflow of verbal abuse a flicker of hope appeared, suggesting that a global settlement was not beyond reach after all, when two of the counsels for the class action

---

[15] *L'Hebdo*, no. 29, July 16, 1998.

[16] *Le Temps*, July 23, 1998.

plaintiffs, Edward Fagan and Robert Swift, along with the representatives of the World Jewish Congress announced that they would lower their claims if the Swiss government was willing to contribute to a global settlement. Mention was also made of the possibility to reach a partial settlement with the banks.

After a further two-day round of very intense negotiations, an agreement was thus finally reached by the various protagonists on August 12, 1998, under the authority of Federal Judge Edward Korman.[17] Under the agreement the Swiss banks accepted to pay a total of 1.25 billion dollars (some 1.8 billion Swiss francs) to Holocaust survivors and the heirs of victims. In return it was agreed that all class action suits against the Swiss banks, including the Swiss National Bank would be dropped. The agreement also settled the dormant accounts issue. Finally, it foreclosed any future legal action against the Swiss government or companies and the lifting of any present or future economic sanctions against Switzerland. The agreement required the banks to pay an installment of 250 million dollars in the first 90 days, and the rest over a period of three years. However, the agreement did not cover the dormant insurance policies. This issue will therefore require an additional payment by the sixteen European insurance companies currently facing a legal challenge over the matter.

The agreement was met with relief on all sides, both by the Jewish organizations and the plaintiffs, and by Swiss business and politicians as well as the U.S. government. However, Swiss public opinion and some political parties were much less happy with the agreement, especially because of the conditions in which the agreement was reached.

---

[17] Settlement Before the Honorable Edward R. Korman, United States District Judge, United States District Court, Eastern District of New York. United States Courthouse, Brooklyn, New York, August 1998.

But even though the agreement was unable to heal all wounds on either side, it had definitively closed the two-year crisis – despite a series of minor incidents causing additional tensions in the next couple of months. For example, Switzerland expressed sharp criticism of Israeli Prime Minister Benyamin Netanyahou when he personally decorated several of Switzerland's most virulent attackers (e.g. World Jewish Congress chairman Edgar Bronfman and Senator D'Amato) in November 1998. Likewise there were renewed tensions between the Swiss bank managers and the Volcker Committee auditors when the latter controlled the Swiss banks' wartime archives. But these incidents were unable to prolong the crisis as the Jewish organizations had all but ended pressure on Switzerland with the signing of the global agreement in August 1998. However, one thing the agreement did not put to an end was Switzerland's search of the full truth on the country's wartime doings, research which remains in the ongoing.

Chapter two

Switzerland in the eye of the storm

Switzerland was hurtled without pity into the eye of the storm raging over the re-examination of the most wrenching years of the century and the Holocaust. It is true that as early as the mid '90s several other countries too were called into question over their commercial ties with Nazi Germany (Spain, Portugal, Turkey and Sweden), their attitude towards Jewish refugees (the United Kingdom and the United States), and for dragging their feet on restoring the rights of Jews (France, Belgium, etc.).

But beyond any doubt it was Switzerland that was bearing the brunt of the criticism and pressure. It was Switzerland that was the butt of Senator D'Amato's most virulent blasts. Switzerland was at the center of Under Secretary Stuart Eizenstat's critical spring 1997 report. Again it was Switzerland that was singled out at the London Conference on Nazi Gold in December 1997. Switzerland was the country the U.S. survivors of the Holocaust and the victims' heirs brought class action suits against. Yet again Switzerland was the country the Jewish organizations, with the World Jewish Congress in the front line, leveled their unending attacks at. Finally, it was Switzerland several U.S. States and cities threatened to boycott.

What is so unusual and intriguing about this overflow of criticism and pressure is that they were directed at a country of which two thirds of the population speak German but that had never been an ally of Nazi Germany, nor participated in the devilish plan to exterminate the Jewish nation. It is fitting to bring these facts to mind. Here, in the very heart of a continent brought under the sway of a criminal regime was a country that remained, by dint of much sacrifice, an island of freedom and democracy. Even in its most serious mistakes Switzerland acted no worse than any other European country. Quite the contrary!

This is not to say that Switzerland need not search its past for any errors it committed. But in no way can this justify the bitter attacks so relentlessly launched on the country throughout the crisis.

Still, it will be unwise to try to absolve Switzerland by showing that other countries have done the same or worse things. It is not by pointing at the faults of others that one's own will disappear. But when people pretend to be searching for justice and truth, the very least is to treat all parties equally. This has obviously not been the case for Switzerland. Worse, the naked truth is that Switzerland was the focus of an all-out libel campaign.

Double standards

What was so disturbing was that while many countries were involved by the search for truth on issues like wartime policies on Jewish refugees, relations with Nazi Germany and dormant accounts, Switzerland was to be singled out for criticism. Perhaps even more disturbing was the fact that the United States, from where came the fiercest attacks on Switzerland, did not have a clean slate itself. Even Israel could be seriously faulted with regard to dormant accounts of Holocaust victims.

This book will in the coming chapters put a finger on the serious mistakes and lack of humanity of some Swiss banks in the dormant accounts issue. But no amount of mistakes Switzerland made can make void the claim that the country is far from being the only one where dormant accounts were or to this day remain a problem.

The first country that comes to mind is Israel itself. In the 1930s a number of European Jews deposited assets in banks in Palestine, which at that time was under British mandate. Since such assets belonged to its enemy, Britain seized them when World War II broke out. At first Britain seized only the assets of Jews living in Germany, but as the Third Reich conquered larger and larger parts of Europe, it also confiscated the assets of Jews living in any occupied country. After the war, Britain transferred the confiscated assets to the fledgling State of Israel. The Israeli government, however, never published a list of these accounts. After ten years Israeli banks should normally transfer to the Israeli Ministry of Justice the amounts deposited on dormant accounts. But this is not a binding rule, each bank being free to adopt its own policy on the issue. According to Ministry of Justice administrator general Chmonel Tzur, the "banks have a large number of dormant accounts. To date only a couple of banks have transferred the amounts involved. We have sent the others a large number of dunning letters, but they are not very forthcoming."[18] Thus, citing bank secrecy, the banks refused to publish a list of dormant accounts. According to Chmonel Tzur "the banks are not willing to make a real effort to trace the owners. (...) Look at what the banks would have to pay in interest on accumulated capital!"[19]

---

[18] Interview with the *Nouveau Quotidien*, October 15, 1997.
[19] Interview with the *Financial Times*, December 2, 1997.

Not before November 1997 did the Knesset Financial Committee ask that the banks send a list of their dormant accounts to Mr. Tzur's department. Finally, in June 1998, a bill was tabled in the Knesset under which the Israeli banks would be forced to lift bank secrecy on an estimated 10,000 dormant accounts, some of which belonged to Jewish Holocaust victims. Still, no international commission or accounting firms sifting through bank archives were foisted on Israel, as was the case with Switzerland.

What is so surprising is the fact that neither the World Jewish Congress nor the Jewish Agency, that were so inflexible with the Swiss banks, had put any pressure on the Israeli banks over the past few decades. When questioned in December 1997 on the Israeli banks' refusal to part with bank secrecy, Jewish Agency president Avraham Burg answered that, "for the moment the Israeli banks do not cooperate in this issue. So far no-one has spoken to me about the matter. As soon as that happens, I will obviously go about the problem in the same way as with Switzerland, for example."[20]

This argument is specious. If one requires others to be forthcoming, just and humane, but fails to apply the same principles to oneself, or with less determination, one loses credibility. Needless to say that in the light of their lack of determination, the credibility rating of the Israeli government, and especially the Jewish organizations in this matter is not very high.

What further impairs Israel's credibility is the fact that the Israeli issue goes far beyond dormant accounts. The country also has a serious problem with unclaimed real estate. European Zionist Jews had bought land or property in Palestine before World War II. Some purchased real estate for investment

---

[20] Interview with the *Weltwoche*, December 4, 1997.

purposes, but others planned to one day emigrate to Palestine. The administrator general of the Israeli Ministry of Justice holds a list of unclaimed properties. Some properties have been transferred to the Jewish National Fund and are now managed by municipalities. Others have been expropriated by the State.

However, not before September 1997 did the administrator general finally publish a list featuring the names of 10,000 owners of 4,000 unclaimed units of land or properties. Why, may one wonder again, did the Israeli government take half a century to publish the list? The official excuse was that government feared that fraudsters would claim ownership, a reason that is not worth a second thought! It must be noted that here too the Jewish organizations never put any real pressure on Israel to settle the matter. Neither have the Jewish Agency or the World Zionist Organization, which owns the Zionist archives, ever opened the archives to settle the problem. The true reason for the Israeli government's belated action must thus unquestionably be traced back to public pressure and the publication by Switzerland of lists of dormant accounts.

But whether the Israeli government really intends to restore the unclaimed properties to their legal owners is another question. According to some estimates they are worth several billion dollars. Some observers in Israel also believe the lists to be incomplete, covering as little as 10% of all unclaimed real estate. Moreover, restitution will in all likelihood be long-drawn-out. This was the case in Switzerland before the outbreak of the dormant accounts crisis, and was the cause for much sharp, often justifiable criticism by the Jewish organizations. But what complicates matters even more in Israel is the fact that the claimants must prove that they are the legal owners by producing the registered number of the claimed property. According to Mr. Tzur this will be very hard since the land register may not be consulted.[21]

But Israel is not the only other country faced with a dormant accounts problem. During the pre-war fascist era, many Jews transferred large amounts to countries other than Switzerland, e.g. the United States and the United Kingdom. A share of these assets have never been returned to the heirs of Holocaust victims, either because they had been confiscated during the war by the countries in which they were deposited, or because the banks have never made any real effort to recover the heirs.

There is ample reason to believe that a large number of European Jews who later fell victim to the Holocaust have in the pre-war years deposited assets in the United States, often via Switzerland. A share of these assets have without doubt been repatriated to Switzerland after the war (there must still be proof of these transfers in the U.S.). But it is also reasonable to expect that a large percentage of the assets have never been repatriated to Switzerland after the war and to this day remain in the U.S.

The existence of dormant accounts in the U.S. led many to criticize America for not practicing what it was preaching to Switzerland, i.e. demanding that Switzerland launch large-scale searches of dormant accounts and their owners but not committing itself to such searching.

However, despite such criticism it was not before April 29, 1998, that the U.S. Senate Banking Committee finally passed a bill on the setting up of a Presidential Advisory Committee with a mandate to search for dormant accounts of Holocaust victims in the U.S.[22] This Banking Committee, so slow to im-

[21] Interview with the *Nouveau Quotidien, op. cit.*

[22] The Senate unanimously passed the law on May 1, 1998 (D'Amato/Leach bill).

plement measures in the United States, was chaired by the self-same Senator D'Amato, the relentless whip of Swiss Banks who, since 1996, had been unceasingly attacking the Swiss Banks in an effort to have them open up their own archives and restitute all Holocaust assets they held. Had Mr. D'Amato and the U.S. passed such a bill two years before, they would certainly have been more credible.

What is even more striking is the fact that the D'Amato/Leach bill sets December 31, 1999, as the deadline for the Commission's search for dormant assets in the U.S. This slowness contrasts sharply with Mr. D'Amato's incessant criticism of Switzerland's perceived slow search and restitution of dormant assets. Most of the Holocaust survivors are very old, and time therefore precious to them. It is all too easy to criticize others. What is harder is to do better than they when one is faced with the same problems...

The United Kingdom too had to deal with dormant accounts of Holocaust victims. For months there was a fierce debate over the British government's wartime confiscation of German Jewish and Third Reich assets deposited in the country. Finally, in April 1998, the government decided to award compensation to Nazi survivors and allocate an initial amount of two million pounds to a special compensation fund.

France too was involved. In fact, it still has to deal with the painful issue of the Vichy government's expropriation between 1942 and 1944 of Jewish assets deposited in French banks. In France the problem is compounded by the government's wartime looting of Jewish properties and works of art.

Another example of double standards was the singling out of Switzerland for criticism in the Jewish refugee issue. Switzerland's policy on Jewish refugees was no different than those of other Western democracies like the United States, the United Kingdom, France, Denmark, Belgium, the Netherlands or Sweden. In many respects Switzerland's policy was even less restrictive.

It was pointed out, and with reason, that Switzerland had taken in as little as 29,000 Jews by 1944. But measured as a percentage of the local population, other democracies, the U.S. to begin with, have over the same period taken in much less.[23]

Switzerland is also accused of having decided not to provide public funds for Jewish refugees, requiring that either they themselves or the Jewish community cover their expenses. This was a gross mistake. But it would be dishonest to pretend that this policy was limited to Switzerland. The U.S. and Britain adopted the same attitude. The U.S. administration, for example, required that all refugees applying for an immigrant visa prove that their income would be sufficient to support themselves, or that they obtain a financial guarantee from a family member living in the U.S. This condition, called the LPC clause (*likely to become a public charge*), was devised to ensure that visa applicants would not become, even a long time after arriving in the U.S., dependent on welfare. Thus any U.S. Jewish associations that could not produce financial guarantee for immigrant Jews saw their visa applications flatly refused. By far the largest part of German applications for visas between 1933 and 1940 involved Jews. Many of those the U.S. turned down were to fall victim to the Holocaust...

As for the United Kingdom, it required that the British Jewish community formally undertake to cover all settlement and maintenance expenses for Jewish refugees from Germany.

At the 1938 Evian Conference in France, the Western democracies also reconfirmed that no country at the conference would have to meet the settlement expenses of involuntary emigrants.

---

[23] For more statistics, see chapter 5.

The end of the war did not spell an immediate improvement of the lot of Jews either. The 800,000 concentration camp survivors in Germany, most of whom were Jews, were left cooped up in the camps, some of them for up to three years! Jewish refugees from the camps were refused access to the United States. And for almost three years after the war they were not allowed to emigrate to Israel either. As if this and the terrible camp conditions they had to endure were not enough, they also had to put up with the anti-Semitism of the American troops.

These examples go to show that there was no reason to single out Switzerland for criticism and pressure. Still, Switzerland, like any other country, should search out its past to put right any wrongs or mistakes it had made.

In the same vein, one has to admit that the Swiss are not used to being called into question. They are perhaps a little sensitive to international criticism. Also, Switzerland and America, the source of most of the criticism and actions against Switzerland, have different (some say opposite) ways of doing things. The Swiss are slow to act. Before taking and implementing decisions they gather all the necessary information. Americans, on the contrary, like to make a show of things, make bold statements and are quick to aggressively turn on the pressure. As World Jewish Congress Vice-President Gerhardt Riegner points out, the two countries have two very different political cultures: "The American way is aggressive: you get angry and right from the start question everything. But in Switzerland everything is based on compromises. Everyone is taken into account, and from the outset all know there will be compromises. This had made for a lot of misunderstandings between the two countries."[24]

[24] *Tages-Anzeiger* of January 20, 1998.

Mr. Riegner is undoubtedly right. The differences of culture, world views and ways of acting have certainly contributed to the crisis. But this does not account for everything. Is does not, for example explain why Switzerland has been hounded down so relentlessly during the crisis.

In fact, Switzerland was so abundantly criticized and the methods used against it so elaborate, that one cannot but speak of a full-blown smear campaign.

Smear campaign

Since spring 1996, but especially during 1997 and the first part of 1998, Switzerland was to be the focus of ever sharper criticism from Senator D'Amato and several Jewish organizations (World Jewish Congress, Jewish Agency, Simon Wiesenthal Center) as well as the U.S. Under Secretary of State, Stuart Eizenstat. Very often their aggressive criticism was based on judgments showing little regard for facts and careful investigation. But thanks to a shrewd media campaign and strings of explosive sound bites, they were given much media coverage. American public opinion soon turned against Switzerland. For example, Senator D'Amato and the World Jewish Congress made a habit of announcing that they have discovered devastating new documents against Switzerland. Most of the time, however, the documents turned out to have been known for a long time and were in no way propping up the sensational accusations leveled at Switzerland. So often avid for sensational news, the media was quick to relay these so-called "discoveries" and serious accusations as is. But when the lack of novelty or aptness of the information would become obvious only a few days later, the media would have no or very little appetite left to publish unsensational corrections.

Some Jewish organizations also made completely false accusations based on no proof of whatsoever. But the extravagance of the accusations caught the attention of the media. There were thus rumors being spread of several billions worth of dormant accounts in the Swiss banks; of Nazi Gold, i.e. gold stolen by the Third Reich that the Swiss banks (first in line the Swiss National Bank) have been keeping illegally in their safes ever since the war; allegations that the Swiss government had basically put itself under the Nazis' heel and that most Swiss had been Nazi supporters; rumors that wartime refugee camps in Switzerland were just as bad as Nazi concentration camps; and affirmations that Swiss trading with the Third Reich had helped Germany to prolong its war effort for several years.

Such talk was being spread around in what can effectively be termed a propaganda campaign led by a handful of American and British newspapers.[25] The *New York Times* is an example. As early as 1996 it openly espoused the theories of the World Jewish Congress. Over the next two years it often carried articles that violently took Switzerland to task while grossly misrepresenting the facts. At one stage it even claimed that some dormant assets had been turned over to Swiss citizens! It was against false accusations like this that the Swiss ambassador spoke out at a press conference in Washington on October 30, 1996.[26] In May 1997, a feature article of the *New York Times* even demanded that the Clinton administration freeze Swiss assets in the United States if Switzerland was not willing to pay its "debts". The newspaper also on several occasions violently

---

[25] Faith Whittlesey, former U.S. ambassador to Switzerland, spoke of this as an "American press trial." See her impassioned article in defense of Switzerland, entitled "La Suisse en jugement" (Switzerland on trial), in the *Journal de Genève*, July 21, 1997.

[26] For a report on this press conference, see the Neue Zürcher Zeitung of November 1, 1996.

criticized Swiss neutrality, describing it as "moral deceit". When one reads through the readers letters section of the *New York Times*, one cannot but note that, during the two crisis years, the editor has filtered out almost all stories sent in by Jews grateful to Switzerland for wartime protection. This contrasts sharply with other American or foreign dailies which carried a large number of Jewish letters of thanks to Switzerland.

Another large east coast newspaper, the *Washington Post*, also at times carried surprisingly aggressive articles, projecting the old ackamarackus of a money-grubbing Switzerland. *Old Crimes*, Jim Hoagland's article of May 25, 1997, is an example. Basing his allegations on the Eizenstat report, Mr. Hoagland grossly misrepresented the Nazi Gold issue, claiming that "long after the war the Swiss banks were still clinging to Nazi Gold deposits looted from the gold reserves of other nations and the bodies of Holocaust victims." This book provides proof[27] of the fact that it is a base falsification to speak of "Nazi gold deposits," term which would mean that Switzerland was in possession of a secret Nazi treasure the Nazis deposited in Swiss banks. Nazi Gold has never been *deposited* in Switzerland. Switzerland *bought* gold from the Reichsbank. Such purchases were part of Switzerland's financial and economic transactions with Germany. Mr. Hoagland also attacked Switzerland's neutrality, providing a distorted reading of the Eizenstat report. He thus claimed the experts of Mr. Eizenstat's office (he meant the U.S. Department of State historians led by William Slany) "have cleverly taken apart the Swiss argument that the country's actions were motivated by neutrality and fear of a Nazi invasion. The Swiss evasion was all about money, not survival." Continuing his attack on Swiss neutrality, Mr. Hoagland even stated that "the world has long encouraged the Confederation

[27] See chapter 5.

to use its neutrality as a veil to not have morality and the punishment of the law interfere in its transactions with other countries and their richest citizens. Switzerland is an international creation *(sic)*, a haven for bank secrecy, a luxury playground for tourists and the house or home base of the international officials of the United Nations and other world organizations. Efficiency and anonymity are the only values encouraged in this environment." Such caricature could make one smile...were it not for the fact that these views have caused serious damage to the image of Switzerland in the United States.

The smear campaign at times was the height of virulence and crudeness. For example, *U.S. News and World Report* editor in chief, Mortimer B. Zuckerman, at one point wrote that the Swiss are "greedy, profiteers, money launderers, fences, thieves, looters and liars."[28]

In the United Kingdom neither the government nor the City put any pressure on Switzerland. But a faction in the press did to some extent join the smear campaign mounted by the U.S. east coast newspapers. In a report on Nazi Gold, the *Sunday Times* even took aggressiveness and bad taste to a new height by publishing a photomontage showing Auschwitz's front gate and its dreadful 'Arbeit macht frei' Nazi slogan opening on, not as one would expect the sinister rows of barracks, but Switzerland's idyllic Alpine scenery. The caption read: "Blood money. For half a century, Switzerland's cuckoo clocks and cowbells have hidden a terrible secret. Tom Bower begins the full story of its conspiracy to back Hitler and profit from the Holocaust."[29]

Such was the vulgar and sensational way in which the *Sunday Times* announced Tom Bower's survey. In a book en-

---

[28] *U.S. News and World Report*, June 22, 1998.
[29] *Sunday Times*, March 9, 1997.

titled, *Blood money. The Swiss, the Nazis and the looted Billions,*[30] Mr. Bower further elaborated on his survey of Nazi Gold. The book stood in the tradition of all smear campaigns, damning, as it were, Switzerland in a way more evocative of defamation than precise, reasoned analysis. It lacked the necessary quest for truth on Switzerland's mistakes and wrongs. And the true wrongs there were, were not balanced by the historic, economic and political context of the time. Finally, Mr. Bower stumbled into the pitfalls of generalizations and quantum leaps in logic.

The same pattern of defamation surfaced in the caricatural image of Switzerland Claude Mossé puts on display in his book *Ces Messieurs de Berne: 1939-1945* (These Gentlemen from Bern: 1939-1945).[31] In it Mr. Mossé, who has worked in Switzerland for 40 years, concocts an unconvincing analysis of the Nazi Gold and dormant accounts issues, peppering it with a series of aggressive statements against Switzerland. He thus states that Switzerland's wartime vices of, as he sees it, ill-will and doublespeak are still the defining elements of Switzerland, the Swiss and political and economic life in the country fifty years after the war.

But the lowest point in the smear campaign against Switzerland was reached on June 18, 1997, when the BBC broadcast the documentary Nazi Gold. The aim of the film was to prove that Switzerland's wartime actions were scarcely better than those of Nazi Germany. A statement by a Jewish Member of the British Parliament in the film also aptly summarizes the film's aim: "The Swiss should find out what bastards their grandfathers were!" To get this point across, the film director did not hesitate to use every device of manipulation and mon-

[30] London, Macmillan, 1997.
[31] Paris, Stock, 1997.

tage available, resorting to the tried and tested techniques of propaganda used by Goebbels himself. As Swiss ambassador to the United Kingdom François Nordmann so aptly put it in a letter of protest to the director general of the BBC: "The unilateral way in which were treated and mounted the stories, which in themselves are truly distressing, to prove a preconceived theory, is a travesty of history and reality (...). The BBC has decided to present a scandalous scenario that sowed hatred and brought into disrepute a whole country, resorting, as it were, to a style of emotions, insinuations and slander–punctuated with true stories–that Goebbels himself would not have disowned!"[32]

The documentary was proof of such extraordinary ill-will towards Switzerland that it triggered sharp reactions from all sides, even from people or institutions who had no reason to hide the past weaknesses and mistakes of Switzerland. Thus, Zurich film director Richard Dindo, who in 1975 called into question received Swiss historiography with his film "The execution of Ernst S., traitor to the country," called the film an "outright fabrication," adding that "the Swiss have had enough of being insulted by people who do not know anything about their country. (...) Switzerland has been sullied so much that even people like myself now start saying, 'cut the mud!'"[33] Israeli ambassador to Switzerland, Gabriel Padon, also clearly came out against the documentary, stating, "I understand that the Swiss are angry about this polemical BBC documentary on Swiss behavior in World War II. (...) For me it is an anti-Swiss film." [34]

---

[32] Cited by the *Nouveau Quotidien* of July 3, 1997.
[33] *Nouveau Quotidien*, July, 15, 1997.
[34] *Neue Zürcher Zeitung*, September 15, 1997.

Effects of the smear campaign

It is very hard to with certainty determine what the effects of this smear campaign were on the image of Switzerland abroad. But it is safe to make the following observations.

It is indisputable that Switzerland's short-term image has been sullied. The BBC film, for example, has strongly influenced large sectors of foreign public opinion. This comes out very clearly from surveys carried out in the U.S. in the weeks following the broadcast. A Swiss teacher working in the United States cites the following reactions as representative of the many he heard during that time:

"The Swiss have lost any respect that I once had for them. After seeing your program, you have ended any future thoughts I might have had about visiting Switzerland, and I hope many other Americans will do the same.

"The evidence is irrefutable. Swiss individuals collaborated, and indeed provided invaluable financial and manufacturing services for the Nazi war effort. In addition, the Swiss banking community was party to the looting of Jewish property and the embezzlement of Jewish bank accounts.

"The Swiss have obviously become very wealthy on the blood and tears of others.

"I have visited that country many times, however, I will never have anything to do with that nation or its products, banks, or the Red Cross again."[35]

The negative effects of the smear campaign have without a doubt spread so rapidly because the majority of Americans have very superficial knowledge of Switzerland. Some know nothing about the country at all, except for a few clichés (e.g. Heidi, chocolate and watches). Even Senator Barbara Boxer,

---

[35] *Neue Zürcher Zeitung*, July 11, 1997.

one of the foremost members of the Senate banking committee that Senator D'Amato chaired, at one stage during the hearings got mixed up between Switzerland and Sweden, and without batting an eyelid claimed that Switzerland had had no army during World War II.[36]

Over the longer term, the effects of such a campaign are less clear-cut. Public opinion shifts rapidly. Switzerland's overseas image may therefore not suffer too much, though it is still too early to say. But even in the long term it is unlikely that the country will come out of the smear campaign unscathed. Whatever the case, one must remember that the aim of the campaign was not to harm Switzerland's long-term image, but to put pressure on the country and achieve a short-term goal – aim which, no doubt about it, was fully achieved.

Some would say that the effects of the campaign against Switzerland must not be exaggerated, that it mostly came from one country, the United States, and was confined to the American east coast (Washington and New York) and California. The media in the other American States gave very little importance to the crisis and the accusations against Switzerland.

This is no doubt true. Still, even a limited spread of the campaign in the United States holds considerable consequences for Switzerland. Firstly, the U.S. is one of Switzerland's foremost financial and commercial partners. With 35 billion dollars of foreign direct investment, Switzerland is America's seventh largest investor. In 1996, Switzerland exported goods and services to the U.S. for over 11 billion dollars. Secondly, the U.S. is the world's only remaining superpower and its influence, pressure and actions have enormous effect on Switzerland. Thirdly, thanks to the weight of its institutional investors (notably pension funds), the U.S. is one of

[36] *Neue Zürcher Zeitung*, July 5-6, 1997.

the Swiss banks' most important clients. Fourthly, and certainly most importantly, it is precisely in New York, Washington and California where America's opinion leaders, most important media and centers of economic and political power are located.

Why was Switzerland alone in the eye of the storm?

One may rightly wonder why Switzerland was singled out in the dormant accounts, the Nazi Gold and the Jewish refugee crises; why the criticism and attacks on Switzerland were so sharp and so concentrated; and what were the true reasons for a smear campaign? Before answering these questions one must admit that Switzerland's actions in the war and over the past fifty years were not beyond reproach. They do require an explanation. But this holds true for many other countries too, and even more so, as we have pointed out. There is therefore no apparent reason for Switzerland's singling out for criticism and claims for compensation. So, precisely what caused Switzerland to be alone in the eye of the storm?

There is no simple answer to this question. The reasons are varied and complex. Finding a single answer to the question is very convenient, but also intellectually dishonest. Above all, one must guard against the same type of simplistic and abusive approaches used by those this book accuses of a gross lack of meticulousness in judging Switzerland's past.

The extraordinary concentration of attacks first of all arose from the attitude of Switzerland's own banks in the first phases of the crisis. The Big Three Swiss banks – which are much more to be blamed than the smaller banks – and the Swiss Bankers' Association were incapable of perceiving the nature and scale of the issue. So secure in their legal certainties and arrogance were the upper echelons of these banks that they committed the most unbelievable errors of judgment. This afforded the Jewish organizations excellent pretexts and – it must be admitted – even valid reasons to raise their demands and launch a full-scale media and political campaign against Switzerland.

It is indisputable that the big Swiss banks were unable, at the beginning of the crisis, to take adequate stock of the errors made on dormant accounts up to that point. So blinded were they by their legalistic view of bank secrecy, that they made the fatal error of choosing to argue instead of admitting to their mistakes and changing their attitude. Within the framework of the Swiss Bankers' Association, they did accept to implement a few measures on the search for dormant accounts. But what they did not understand was that their action should not only have involved legal but also human aspects.

Also, the banks' lack of humanity in some cases went hand in hand with extreme arrogance and catastrophic communication policies.

The Swiss Bankers' Association was so taken up in procedural matters, that for a long time it failed to provide answers to the international community and seemed insensitive to the personal problems and damage suffered by the victims. The Association's August 1995 decision to adopt new bank directives on unclaimed assets was a praiseworthy move. It was also a wise thing when the Association asked the Bank Ombudsman Foundation and the ombudsman for the Swiss banks (two institutions totally independent of the banks) to set up an Inquiry Office. But these necessary initiatives could not cancel out the coldness that had characterized the Association for so many decades, neither could they make up for the lack of communication skills of the banks' managers. Most of all, the initiatives did nothing to improve the bank managers' inadequate perception of the true scale of the looming crisis.

The beginning of 1998 saw a new team of managers taking office at the secretariat of the Swiss Bankers' Association. With them came a series of new policies. But it was too late to put right past mistakes. Moreover, the problems the Association made were not linked to the secretariat only. The Association is far from the powerful lobby group many people hold it to be. It has few means and has long been marked by amateurism. The weak structure of the Association really reflects the internal divisions of the Swiss banking sector. It has never been able to unite under a strong leadership capable of imposing a clear policy instead of getting bogged down in legal and procedural issues.

Some of the managers of the UBS also added to the tensions through a series of disastrous declarations. For example, the chairman of the bank's board of directors, Robert Studer, qualified the amounts in the dormant accounts at the bank as "peanuts".[37] It is only understandable that the Holocaust survivors and heirs felt this to be an insult. Robert Holzach, UBS honorary chairman, blundered even more when he in an interview with the American press made remarks that could be interpreted as anti-Semitic. Not before November 1997 did UBS CEO Mathis Cabialavetta formally admit to mistakes his bank had made in the dormant accounts issue and apologize for the bank managers' insensitive declarations. Things were definitely moving in the right direction, but it was perhaps too little too late.

The Union Bank of Switzerland also made serious mistakes in the Meili affair – the night watch who had saved the

[37] KABEL, Marcus, "Swiss Banks denies holding sums from Holocaust victims", Reuters, February 23, 1996.

archives an archivist was at the point of destroying. The destruction of the archives would have breached the December 13, 1996, Federal Decree on the Protection of Archives dating back to 1920-1950. The fact that the bank managers and spokesperson claimed that the documents Mr. Meili had saved were of no importance, thus playing down their responsibility, and pressed ahead with charges of infringement of bank secrecy against him only worsened matters with the Jewish organizations. When Mr. Meili emigrated to the United States, claiming that he was threatened in his country, it was easy for Senator D'Amato to present him as a martyr persecuted by the Swiss banks and government and to obtain asylum for him in the U.S. Suffice it to quote Mr. D'Amato's press declaration: "Mr. Meili should be viewed as a hero not a criminal. His actions in preventing the destruction of evidence are courageous and serve the cause of justice for the victims and survivors of the Holocaust and their families. In April, we learned that Mr. Meili had been fired. This was outrageous! It is a stain upon the victims' memory that a young man who saved records to help their cause has now become a victim. Unfortunately Christoph received hundreds of death threats forcing him to flee his native land. Thankfully we were able to pass legislation providing sanctuary to Christoph and his family here in the U.S."[38] Mr. D'Amato's exploitation of the Meili case finally came full circle in January 1998 with Mr. Meili's lawyer, Edward Fagan, lodging a claim for 2.56 billion dollars against the Union Bank of Switzerland.

---

[38] Internet site of Senator D'Amato.

Swiss isolation

Two other reasons for the scale of attacks on Switzerland are the small size of the country and its isolation in Europe and the world. Switzerland's action in the international arena is obviously limited by its size. But the relative weakness of a small country like Switzerland does not arise from geographic and demographic factors only. Economics are also an important factor. Despite the fact that Switzerland is a very rich country and possesses one of the world's foremost financial centers, its financial strength is not backed up by a large economy such as is the case with the United States and, to a lesser extent, Britain, Germany and France. Switzerland is thus unshielded from international pressure, and has very little means of counterattacking or rectifying its international image.

But Switzerland's international isolation is an even more important factor than its small size in explaining why the country came under such concentrated and sustained fire.

In many senses Switzerland is an open country. Due to its lack of natural resources, it had to open up its economy to international trade very early. Thanks to this policy, Switzerland developed strong industrial and service sectors. A large percentage of the Swiss economy can thus be said to be open to the outside world. But Switzerland has never joined the European Union. European integration is an economic, political and social process. Lack of membership in the EU therefore isolates Switzerland from the rest of Europe not only in an economic sense, but also politically and socially. True, Switzerland is a member of several other European institutions such as the Council of Europe and the Organization for Security and Cooperation in Europe, as well as a large number of scientific and technological organizations such as the European Space Agency and CERN (European Organization for

Nuclear Research), etc. But the leading institution in Europe today, especially since the end of the Cold War, is the European Union.

The increasing isolation of Switzerland in Europe and the world is cause for concern because it results in the country becoming more and more vulnerable. The Swiss government is not unaware of the danger of the country's marginalization in Europe and the world due to its absence from leading political and collective security organizations such as the European Union and the United Nations. Hence the government's admission, in its *Report on Switzerland's Foreign Economic Policy in the 90s*, that "in the current global context, Switzerland's absence from international organizations is bound to harm its medium- and long-term interests as well as its capacity for development; and may even weaken its position in the global arena."[39] In 1997, Swiss Federal Councilor Flavio Cotti also pointed out that, "the countries outside international networks are facing a growing handicap. One characteristic of such networks is the systematic nature of exchange. This favors cooperation, reduces divergences and increases mutual understanding."[40]

But the Swiss government has still not wholly understood where isolation is taking the country. This is especially true for the country's defense policy. Neutrality has already isolated Switzerland, and indeed is increasing its isolation. If nothing else, the Nazi Gold crisis should be proof that it is not in the medium- or long-term, as the Swiss government opined, that Switzerland risks seeing its international role weakened. It is already happening. International weakening is the direct result

---

[39] *Rapport sur la politique économique extérieure de la Suisse dans les années 90* (Report on Switzerland's Foreign Economic Policy in the 90s), Bern, November 29, 1993, p. 14.
[40] *Le Nouveau Quotidien*, May 15, 1997.

of Switzerland's international isolation. This situation is compounded by a growing divide in Swiss public opinion on what the founding principles of Swiss society and Switzerland's role in the world should be. This identity crisis unfortunately only increases Switzerland's vulnerability *vis-à-vis* external pressure.

If Switzerland had been a member of the European Union, it would certainly not have been singled out to such an extent in the dormant accounts and Nazi Gold issues. Small countries in the European Union are to a large extent shielded from external political and financial pressure thanks to a kind of EU solidarity, the growing integration of the EU members economies, and the single European currency. It has become almost impossible to affect one country without affecting the whole European Union.

It was thus because of Switzerland's small size, and especially because of its international isolation that the Jewish organizations, drawing on the United States' dominant position, succeeded in their violent smear campaign against the country. The organizations' best chance of success was certainly to focus on weak and isolated Switzerland. Hence their fierce horse-trading. It was clear to them that once they broke the weakest link in the chain, it would become easier to take on countries less likely to give in. With the large concessions they hoped to wring from the Swiss, they would be able to claim similar amounts of compensation from the banks or companies of other countries. And precisely this is busy happening. In the weeks that followed the signing of the global agreement with the Swiss banks, pressure, again backed up by class action suits in the U.S., switched to banks and companies in Germany, Austria, France and elsewhere. For example, the World Jewish Congress immediately started to violently press Germany's Deutsche Bank to pay compensation to Holocaust victims. Pressure intensified in January 1999 when the World Jewish

Congress threatened to launch international sanctions against the Deutsche Bank in the same way it had imposed them on Switzerland. In another pressure action the World Jewish Congress opposed a merger between the Deutsche Bank and Bankers Trust, an American bank.

One wonders whether this strategy was thought up by the World Jewish Congress and its allies, most notably Mr. D'Amato, right from the start, or whether it was forged gradually by the events and Switzerland's weakness. It is hard to answer. It was probably a mix of the two. Switzerland must have been identified as a weak spot right from the start. And most likely Swiss behavior during the crisis allowed to increase pressure and fine-tune a strategy that was working very well. This brings us to another factor that fueled the attacks, namely the inability of the Swiss government to right from the beginning correctly read events and forestall the crisis.

The part the Swiss government played

Despite signs heralding tensions as early as 1995, the Swiss government was for the most part unaware of the looming crisis. The government and the administration did not comprehend just how high the stakes were when the Swiss banks were first called into question on the dormant accounts issue, Swiss wartime Nazi Gold purchases, and Swiss policy on Jewish refugees. Neither did they comprehend how fragile Switzerland was, especially on account of the country's isolation. The government also overlooked the importance of a united approach on the moral issue, for example by accepting full responsibility for Switzerland's past wrongs while at the same time preparing to face up to claims that, as it turned out, would be closer to blackmail than an honest search for truth.

These failures led to Switzerland adopting the defensive attitude of a country unwilling to face its past, and only served to pour fuel to the fire of the Jewish organizations.

These shortcomings also explain why the Swiss government was unable to define a true strategy. Its behavior was reactive. It lacked a clear-cut goal. Switzerland came across as passive. As Ambassador Thomas Borer, head of the Swiss task force, later admitted, Switzerland was taking a beating without even knowing that it was in a boxing match.[41] On several occasions the Swiss government also gave the impression that it did not know what to do. For example, the government and the Parliament could not find common ground on Swiss National Bank participation in the Special Fund. No Federal Decree on the Special Fund was therefore passed, preventing Switzerland from sending a clear signal as to the country's desire to put right its record on purchases of looted gold. The Swiss National Bank was thus left to take a decision on its own. This in turn fueled demands by the Jewish organizations and U.S. politicians for the government to directly participate in a global agreement.

The failure of the Swiss government to publicly assume moral responsibility (e.g. through a strongly worded statement of regret) for all Swiss mistakes toward Holocaust victims, and then to powerfully oppose – even counter-attack if necessary – efforts to denigrate, put under pressure or blackmail the country, emasculated the government, robbing it of an effective communication strategy. Switzerland was all the time on the defense. All this was highly counter-productive in terms of restoring Switzerland's image abroad, especially in the United States.

---

[41] *Journal de Genève*, January 10-11, 1998.

The situation was beyond repair. Hiring a U.S. public relations company (for 500,000 dollars per year!), or charging the Swiss embassy in Washington to present a more favorable face of Switzerland to the American public than the one Jewish organizations, such as the World Jewish Congress, were conveying, was to no avail. Switzerland lacked a clear strategy and was perceived to be on the defensive. Once the Jewish organizations gained the upper hand, they were unstoppable. As Ambassador Borer pointed out, "some Jewish organizations are no longer interested in historic data or debating the moral points. All they want is money!"[42]

The Swiss government, banks and companies have in the course of the crisis set up a number of funds or commissions that put them far ahead of other countries (Special Fund, Volcker Committee, Bergier Commission, Swiss Foundation for Solidarity). No other country in the world has done so much in such a short time. But unfortunately for Switzerland, such initiatives were piecemeal. They were reactive, the result of external pressure, not a coherent, active, well-thought-out strategy. They also seemed to be introduced in a rush. The Swiss Foundation for Solidarity, for example, was poorly defined and the source of a lot of confusion. It appeared more like a panic measure designed to assuage external pressure than a well-considered initiative intended to introduce a larger amount of solidarity. The subsequent shilly-shallying of the government on whether to include Holocaust survivors in the Foundation only aggravated an already sorry state of affairs.

The setting up in October 1996 of a special task force in the Federal Department of Foreign Affairs was a step in the right direction as the Swiss diplomatic corps was ill-equipped to face up to Jewish NGOs backed up by some of the highest-

---

[42] *Le Temps*, May 20, 1998.

level politicians in the United States, the world's only remaining superpower. But the task force was set up too late. The crisis was already well under way. Besides, a special task force could bring little benefit if the Swiss government failed, as it did, to provide a strong and clear strategy.

However, credit must be given to the Swiss government for stiffening their stance from the spring of 1998 onwards. It thus refused to participate in a global agreement between the big Swiss banks and the Jewish organizations. This new attitude reflected a high level of disgust in Swiss public opinion and the Swiss Jewish community with the American Jewish organizations and their increasingly arrogant attacks. Again, in the summer of 1998, the Swiss government reacted very firmly to the sanctions decided by several American States after the discussions reached deadlock. As earlier pointed out, the Swiss government – in the person of Ambassador Borer – on July 9, 1998, responded by sending a very tersely worded letter to New York city comptroller Alan Hevesi, denouncing his scandalous, manipulative methods. Swiss president Cotti followed up the letter with a second missive to President Clinton on July 22. In his letter President Cotti pointed out that the boycott was unjustified and illegal, putting the good relations between the two countries at risk. But the stiffened stance of the Swiss government came too late to change a by now almost foregone conclusion of the crisis.

Vulnerable Swiss banks

The vulnerability of Switzerland's Big Three banks also account for the concentration of attacks on Switzerland. Coupled with their affluence, their vulnerability turned them into ideal targets.

The success of the Big Three banks (Union Bank of Switzerland, Swiss Bank Corporation and the Credit Suisse Group) is also their main weakness when it comes to external pressure. When the crisis erupted, of all Swiss banks the Big Three were the ones most actively increasing the share of foreign activities as a percentage of turnover. Quite obviously this also made them more vulnerable to threats to their activities outside Switzerland. This process was part of a policy of banking and financial "deterritorialization," or "territorial discoupling." The running and success of the Big Three banks were thus becoming less and less dependent on Switzerland and more and more so on external actors and factors, such as the attitude of powerful countries like the United States. This process has been strengthened by changing banking conditions in Switzerland itself. The narrower circumscription of bank secrecy in Switzerland, largely due to American pressure, offers an example.

However, the growing involvement of the Big Three banks in international markets came at a price in Switzerland, the banks' home base. The past few years have thus seen more and more Swiss clients becoming very critical of the big banks, pointing out their loss of interest in the national market, especially when it comes to small private clients and small and medium-sized companies.

This is no doubt true. As the Big Three banks became increasingly active in the global arena, they gradually grew less concerned with the small Swiss market. They therefore had no choice but adjust to foreign conditions. Which also explains why they have become vulnerable. Eric Wollman, the right-hand man of Mr. Hevesi, cited this as reason for the exclusion of the UBS from a banking syndicate set up to launch a loan for New York city. In answer to Union Bank of Switzerland in North America chairman Richard Capone, who had said that the UBS was a Swiss bank with Swiss values, Mr. Wollman retorted that "if the UBS wants to be a global player, it cannot put forward its so-called Swiss mentality. It must adjust."[43]

Another way in which the vulnerability of the Big Three banks increased was through their buying up of foreign companies. Their center of gravity thus gradually moved to New York, London or Tokyo. Vulnerability also increased through the taking on of specialists (which lacked on the Swiss labor market), especially to head up foreign subsidiaries. The Credit Suisse Group was by far the most eager of the three banks to reach a quick agreement with the Jewish organizations and class action plaintiffs. Several observers said this was the case precisely because of the weight of Credit Suisse First Boston, an investment bank in the United States, and its largely American management team.

Given the strength of the New York financial market and the importance of the American market for the Big Three banks, it is easy to understand why they were so vulnerable to pressure and attacks on their image in the United States. As Robin Monro-Davies, managing director of IBCA, a London-based credit-rating agency, pointed out: "The Swiss banks are out to grow in the States, and it would hurt them if they were to become pariahs there." [44]

The 1997 Union Bank of Switzerland and Swiss Bank Corporation merger – resulting in the new United Bank of Switzerland (or simply the UBS) – once again revealed the growing weight of foreign bank activities and the vulnerability of the Big Three banks to the American market. The merger was dictated by the limitations of the Swiss market. The two banks' aim was to develop their foreign activities, especially in

---

[43] Interview with *L'Hebdo*, October 30, 1997.

[44] *Business Week*, May 26, 1997.

the United States, and to create a truly global bank capable of taking on any American counterparts in fields like institutional or private fund management, and investment banking. This explains why the new UBS could ill afford to not quickly settle the Holocaust issue. The merger came under strong pressure as soon as it was announced. Senator D'Amato even asked that the American bank authorities withhold approval of the merger as long as a global settlement had not been reached.

The Big Three banks' vulnerability to American pressure for the most part arose from the size of their involvement in institutional fund management. It is easy to understand why. One only need to take a look at the leading part American institutional investors play in global fund management. With American hedge funds accounting for 6,000 billion dollars out of a world fund management market of 8,500 billion dollars, the United States is by far the world's foremost fund manager. No investment bank can therefore afford to ignore the American institutional investors. And as the big Swiss banks found out – to their detriment – the considerable power they wield can be conclusive in events like the dormant accounts crisis.

All these factors make it easy to understand why the Big Three banks were so concerned about the beating their image was taking in the U.S. Faced with the smear campaign against Switzerland and the Swiss banks and the Jewish organizations' determination to obtain a global settlement, the banks before long understood that no amount of searching for dormant accounts could restore their image and credibility. American public opinion was not the real issue. It was the opinion of American economic and political decision-makers that mattered. The banks had to deter institutional hedge fund managers from joining the boycott several U.S. States, New York and other cities were planning on. If institutional fund managers were going to join the boycott, private fund managers would probably be following suit before long. It is hard to say how much such a boycott would have cost the big banks. But it was likely to cut the American funds they managed by several billion dollars, not to mention a cut in the market share growth they were hoping for.

The Swiss financial center and bank secrecy under attack

There may still be another important reason for the attacks on Switzerland. This has to do with a desire to weaken, or even control, the prosperous Swiss financial center and Swiss bank secrecy.

To state this is obviously to venture onto dangerous ground. Here therefore, even more than for other statements made in this book, all observations should be based on rigorous analysis. It is all too easy to fabricate conspiracy theories and find easy scapegoats; which would serve no other purpose than hiding the very real mistakes Switzerland and its banks had made. And when this happens, racism is just one step further down the road.

Misplaced comments, such as those made by former UBS honorary chairman Robert Holzach, must therefore be rejected emphatically. Mr. Holzach branded the crisis as the first step of a Jewish conspiracy to bring the world's leading financial markets under their control.

Another equally defective theory holds the only cause of the crisis to be an American conspiracy (Jews are not the ones blamed in this case) to undermine and bring the Swiss financial center under American control. The aim of this chapter is precisely to show that there is not only one but many reasons for the intensity of attacks on Switzerland.

However, not all explanations of this kind are instances of paranoia. Along with the other reasons, it is not implausible that the crisis was indeed used by a number of financial and political protagonists in the United States to weaken a rival financial center, and especially to undermine Swiss bank secrecy. Switzerland undoubtedly made mistakes in the dormant accounts crisis. The country will also have to revisit the dark areas in its past. But this does not mean that the extraordinary concentration of attacks and pressure on Switzerland was not, at least to some extent, part of an attack on the Swiss financial center.[45]

With hindsight it indeed seems to have been the case. There is much corroborative evidence for such a statement. American pressure and attacks on Swiss bank secrecy started long before the crisis. For decades American calls for greater transparency and their fight against tax evasion and organized crime (especially the laundering of drug money) have brought enormous pressure to bear on Switzerland and Swiss bank secrecy. American pressure was also instrumental in making Switzerland introduce legislation on insider trading in 1988 and, in 1998, revise the penal code on negligent bank monitoring. Such restrictions are gradually hemming in Swiss bank secrecy and have undoubtedly rendered more efficient the fight against organized crime. But the United States still remains very critical of bank secrecy, considering that it favors tax evasion, which is not a penal offense in Switzerland.

But it would be naive to overlook the fact that lofty American arguments conceal the much less noble agenda of sapping the strength of a rival financial center. Bank secrecy, even though it has been scaled down, remains one of the Swiss

---

[45] See Albert A. Stahel's remarks on this subject, in *Schweizer Monatshefte*, no. 11, 1997, p. 6.

banks' strongest marketing arguments. For the world the Swiss financial center is synonymous with bank secrecy.

What aggravated this state of affairs was the ill-will some Swiss banks exhibited during the dormant accounts issue; which in turn triggered great irritation on the New York financial center. Bank secrecy, it was said, has been put on a pedestal in Switzerland, the Swiss have forgotten that bank secrecy serves to protect clients, not banks! The American banking circles thus had a few scores to settle – both figuratively and quite literally – with the Swiss banks. The World Jewish Congress too wanted to "teach the Swiss bankers a few lessons," and use the crisis to call bank secrecy into question. They were greatly helped in this by some American newspapers which published several very biased and strongly worded articles and were certainly hoping to sound the death knell for Swiss bank secrecy.[46] Mr. Bronfman's sharp declarations against Swiss bank secrecy were of the same kind. For example, he was very quick to cry victory when the Swiss banks published the first list of dormant accounts, peremptorily declaring that this now was the end of Swiss bank secrecy.[47] But what Mr. Bronfman seemed to be in the dark about or forget was that the publication of this list was an exception. Swiss bank secrecy was not hanging in the balance. The list was the result of the Swiss Federal Decree of December 13, 1996 on the "historical and legal search for assets deposited in Switzerland after the rise to power of the Nazi regime," as well as a decision taken by the Swiss Federal Banking Commission on June 25, 1997. Moreover, the list included accounts opened before 1945 only. As we can see, Swiss bank secrecy was not in jeopardy at all.

---

[46] For a very good example of this type of writing, see Holman W. Jenkins Jr., "Does the world still need the Swiss?", *Wall Street Journal Europe*, April 23, 1998.
[47] *Le Monde*, July 30, 1997.

But such high-sounding declarations may nonetheless influence the way international opinion perceives the Swiss banking system. They may also contribute to the pressures exerted on Swiss bank secrecy both at the bilateral level with the United States and at the multilateral level in the OECD, for instance, in the context of the struggle against fiscal competition between countries.

Chapter three

The brinkmanship of the Jewish organizations

The World Jewish Congress (WJC) is undoubtedly the major protagonist in the dormant accounts and Nazi Gold crises. Adroitly exploiting some American politicians to further its action, the World Jewish Congress was instrumental in putting Switzerland and the Swiss banks on trial. It was also the World Jewish Congress that kept the pressure rising throughout the crisis. But these facts apart, do we really know who and what the World Jewish Congress is? During the crisis, everyone has heard or read about the World Jewish Congress. With their stunning declarations, World Jewish Congress chairman Edgar Bronfman and other World Jewish Congress leaders often made front-page news. Still, the World Jewish Congress, its origins and aims remain largely unknown to the man in the street.

The World Jewish Congress was founded in Geneva in 1936. It is an international federation of communities and Jewish organizations. Its aim is to represent Jews from all over the world, whatever their political or religious convictions. It unites more than 100 communities grouped into regional areas: North America, Latin America, Europe, Eurasia, Israel and Asia-Pacific Ocean. In 1983 the World Jewish Congress moved its headquarters from Geneva to New York. The Congress also has offices and a research institute in Jerusalem, a European office in Paris, a Latin American office in Buenos Aires, and a UN liaison office in Geneva.

The objective of the World Jewish Congress it to represent Jews with governments and international organizations; to defend the interests and rights of Jews throughout the world; to do so without interfering in the internal affairs of any country. It maintains to be the only lawful representative of Holocaust victims with governments.

The plenary assembly, which is the main decision-making body of the Congress, meets every five years. In the interim period, the governing board of the Congress assumes responsibility for current affairs and decisions.

World Jewish Congress has played a very active role in demanding compensation for Jewish Holocaust victims and promoting Jewish values and customs after World War II. For example, it was instrumental in obtaining compensation from Germany. It was also a key player in the 1952 accord between Germany and Israel. Throughout the world it very effectively lobbied for the rights and interests of Jewish communities, especially in countries that had no or had broken off relations with Israel. It also facilitated the emigration of Jews from the former Soviet Union to Israel. After the fall of communism, it extended its representative role to Jews in the former communist countries, seeking to obtain compensation for assets stolen from Jews in these countries. One of the World Jewish Congress's most publicized actions of the last decades was certainly its campaign against former UN Secretary-General and Austrian President Kurt Waldheim.

In the light of the preceding, the World Jewish Congress can be classified as international NGO acting as a pressure group. What is therefore so curious about the World Jewish Congress is that, despite the extensive media coverage elicited by some of its actions and campaigns, it has never been subjected to any rigorous study, as has been done for almost all other large interest groups. Maybe this lack is due to a form of fear of submitting an organization defending the interests of a people that has suffered so much in the past, and especially in the Holocaust, to the scrutiny of the scientific world. Nonetheless, such research would have allowed to know the World Jewish Congress better. It makes no sense to keep people in the dark as to any part of an organization, no matter how sacred the cause it pretends to defend. Any organization or institution, no matter which one, must be assessed in the light not of what it says it is and does, but of what it really does and is. To critically analyze the World Jewish Congress, as in these paragraphs, in no way calls into question the Holocaust or any of the lawful rights of the Jewish people. Preconceived ideas are an enemy to analysis. But so is obsequiousness. This analysis therefore first and foremost seeks to cast light on a non-governmental organization acting as a pressure group.

Later on in this chapter we will therefore analyze the World Jewish Congress's actions during the dormant accounts and Nazi Gold crises. But a more general aspect of the Congress, i.e. the predominance American Jews have within the Congress, demands attention first.

The official claim of the World Jewish Congress to represent all Jewish communities and organizations throughout the world is far from a reality. When Nahum Goldmann, who had been World Jewish Congress chairman from 1949 to 1977, stepped down and the headquarters of the Congress moved from Geneva to New York, the World Jewish Congress was soon to come under the control of American Jews. Today it is a well-known fact that many Jewish communities, especially in Europe but also in other parts of the world, complain that the World Jewish Congress primarily defends the point of view and interests of American Jews. These communities and many Jews worldwide are also critical of the general attitude, behavior and violent, insensitive methods of the World Jewish Congress.[48]

That the World Jewish Congress status as representative of Jews worldwide is in dispute has very clearly come to the fore in the dormant accounts and Nazi Gold affairs. The Swiss Jewish community was confronted with a barrage of evidence that the World Jewish Congress's actions were not dictated by a desire to represent Jews worldwide, and much less the views, interests and sensibilities of Swiss Jews. On the contrary, the World Jewish Congress actions were all designed, chosen and carried out from within the United States. This caused many Swiss Jews to openly express anger towards the World Jewish Congress, even denying it the right to speak in their name. For example, Sigi Feigel, honorary chairman of the Israeli Community of Zurich and respected member of the Swiss Jewish community remarked that "the World Jewish Congress may well be called 'world congress', but it is firmly in American hands. (...) The autocratic way in which the World Jewish Congress acts against Switzerland reflects a preoccupation with power. In no way whatsoever it takes into consideration Switzerland's 18,000 Jews and their fate."[49] Some members of the Central and Eastern European Jewish communities have even openly started questioning the World Jewish Congress's claim to represent the interests of all Holocaust victims and their heirs.

The World Jewish Congress was the main protagonist in the search for dormant accounts and the questioning of Switzerland's past. But it was not the only Jewish institution in-

---

[48] See also the remarks made by Yvan Dalain in his book *Lettres d'un Suisse à un ami américain. Fonds en déshérence* (Letters from a Swiss to an American friend. Dormant accounts), Vevey, Editions de l'Aire, Switzerland, 1998.
[49] *Tages-Anzeiger*, April 3, 1998.

volved. The Simon Wiesenthal Center in Los Angeles played a very active part too. It was set up in 1977 and has 400,000 members worldwide. Its aim is to perpetuate the memory of the Holocaust and promote human and Jewish rights. The Center has offices in a number of countries, from which it conducts its fight against anti-Semitism. Simon Wiesenthal is a Nazi concentration camp survivor who after the war quit his job as architect to devote his life to tracking down Nazi war criminals. It was to let the memory of his life-long struggle serve as example to future generations that he lent his name to the Center. He personally plays no part in the management of the Center, however.

In June 1997, the Simon Wiesenthal Center organized a conference in Geneva on dormant accounts and art works stolen by the Nazis. The conference also looked into the lack of openness of the tripartite Commission set up by the Allies after the war to redistribute gold stolen by the Nazis.

The Simon Wiesenthal Center also published two surveys that drew a great deal of public attention. The surveys very sharply criticized the Swiss for their attitude toward the Nazis and the treatment they supposedly meted out to Jewish refugees working in the camps the country put up during the war.[50]

Another Jewish organization that played an active role in the crisis was the Jerusalem-based Jewish Agency. Its chairman, Avraham Burg, right from the start of the crisis was one of the sharpest critics of Switzerland. The Jewish Agency for Israel was founded in 1929 by the World Zionist Organization and Jewish representatives from a large number of countries. The

---

[50] SCHOM, Alan Morris, *The Unwanted Guests: Swiss Forced Labor Camps (1940-1944), op. cit.*; SCHOM, Alan Morris, *A Survey of Nazi and Pro-Nazi Groups in Switzerland: 1930-1945*, Los Angeles, Simon Wiesenthal Center, July 1998.

mandate of the Agency was to represent Jews with the British administration in Palestine and other world powers of the time. It also had to work toward the creation of a national homeland for Jews, promote Jewish immigration and set up social services. Upon the creation of Israel in 1948, the State took over most of the Jewish Agency's tasks. Oversight of immigration, however, remained its exclusive responsibility. In 1952 the Israeli government, the World Zionist Organization and the Jewish Agency signed an agreement under which the Agency was also given the task, in conjunction with the World Zionist Organization, of developing Jewish unity. In 1971, however, the Jewish Agency and the World Zionist Organization were separated, and each assigned a separate legal status.

The last Jewish organization involved in the crisis was the World Jewish Restitution Organization. The WJRO was set up in 1993 on an initiative of the World Jewish Congress. It consists of the following nine international Jewish organizations: the World Jewish Congress, the Jewish Agency for Israel, the World Zionist Organization, the American Joint Distribution Committee, the Conference of Jewish Material Claims against Germany, B'nai Brith International, the American Gathering of Jewish Holocaust Survivors, the Center of Organizations of Holocaust Survivors in Israel, and Agudath Israel World Organization (which joined in 1994). The objective of the World Jewish Restitution Organization is to search and claim back the assets confiscated from Jews by the former Eastern European communist governments after World War II. The WJRO returns such belongings to their rightful owners or, when this is no longer possible, turns them over to Jewish charities. Consisting as it does of a number of organizations, the WJRO cannot really be considered a single entity. Besides, the World Jewish Congress, whose chairman, Edgar Bronfman, doubles as chairman of the WJRO, carries more weight within the WJRO than any of the other member organizations.

Organizations looking for recognition

Throughout the crisis all these organizations were driven by the same desire to prove that some European countries, Switzerland first in line, committed wrongs in the war, and had to provide compensation and restitute all dormant accounts. But having had the same aim did not mean that they coordinated their campaigns, quite the contrary. They were actually competing against one another. The stakes were truly high for all of them. They had to prove their value, gain recognition for their actions. It seemed each was trying to go one better than the other. Each was trying to gain favor with Jewish communities, especially with the Holocaust survivors and heirs of victims. Each was trying to cast himself as the most effective and legitimate defender of Jewish rights. The World Jewish Congress right from the start had a clear lead over the others; which made the Jewish Agency and the Simon Wiesenthal Center try even harder to get one up. Jewish Agency chairman Avraham Burg, for example, took an extremely hard line in the global settlement negotiations, obviously only to distance himself from the other Jewish organizations. This was even more obviously the concern of the Simon Wiesenthal Center, which campaigned without ever really cooperating with the World Jewish Congress. This was the case, for example, with the conference it organized in Geneva in June 1997, to which it did not bother to even invite the World Jewish Congress leaders.

Apart from their drive for recognition, the conflicts between the Jewish organizations also had a lot to do with money, and through money, with power. The amount claimed by the organizations and class action plaintiffs was enormous. Who was going to distribute it, and to whom? Such questions led to deep splits between the Jewish movements. There was agreement on the need to give priority to the plaintiffs with justifiable claims. But the bone of contention was how to distribute the large amount not covered by direct claims. Some wanted to disburse it to Holocaust survivors throughout the world in individual or collective payments (through charities). Others wanted to give preference to social, cultural or educational projects for Jews. The political capital the distributors could make was considerable. A desire for money and power thus made a potent recipe for fierce infighting.

Even before a deal was reached with the Swiss banks, some American Jewish plaintiffs challenged the right and soundness of the organizations' distributing and use of any funds they would receive. Gizella Weisshaus, for example, accused the World Jewish Congress and other members of the World Jewish Restitution Organization of improper distribution of Holocaust victim compensation in the past.[51] Ed Fagan, a lawyer representing some 23,000 class action plaintiffs claiming a total of $20bn from the Swiss banks, even charged the World Jewish Congress with advocating a global settlement for the sole purpose of getting money for itself, not for the defense of the victims' rights.[52]

In fact, tensions broke out in the open as early as 1997 over the ways to distribute the 265 million Swiss francs that Switzerland allocated to the Special Fund. Such differences grew much larger and louder after the global deal of August 1998. Now it was the sharing out of $1.25bn that was at stake.

[51] *Nouveau Quotidien*, November 14, 1997.
[52] *Basler Zeitung*, December 4, 1997.

There were sharp differences between the various Jewish movements themselves, as well as between them and the lawyers of the class action plaintiffs in the U.S. The bone of contention, as was mentioned before, involved the sums that would remain once all dormant account holders identified by the Volcker Committee had been paid in full. The remaining amount would still be in excess of $1bn, a huge amount by any standard. This money had to be divided between the class action plaintiffs on the one hand, and social and religious works in the United States, Israel, Europe and the rest of the world on the other. The class action plaintiffs were very unhappy. A few of their lawyers, especially of the Jewish Orthodox community, even accused the World Jewish Congress of wanting to monopolize the funds made available under the global deal just as it had done with the Special Fund.

Such tensions must not be exaggerated. They are largely inevitable. But they do reflect the importance the huge sums had for the Jewish organizations in terms of proving their *raison d'être* and courses of action.

Apart from conflict between the Jewish organizations themselves, there were also a number of incidents reflecting differences of interests between them and the Israeli government. For example, for months on end a sharp disagreement between Israel and the associations of Holocaust survivors was blocking the disbursing of 85m francs of the humanitarian fund to victims in Israel. Israel and the Jewish movements' very different approach to the crisis probably sprung from the fact that the dormant accounts and Nazi Gold affairs were outclassed by much more urgent affairs in Israel. The Israeli government and public opinion thus never became involved in the crisis with the same determination and interest as Jewish public opinion in the United States or the Jewish organizations. Besides, until recently Israel has always sought to maintain good relations with Switzerland, as was very clear during Federal Councilor Flavio Cotti's visit to that country in May 1998. This was again confirmed by a piece of information published in *Ha'aretz*, an Israeli newspaper, that sparked a bitter controversy shortly before Mr. Cotti's visit. According to the newspaper, Israeli ambassador to Switzerland, Itzhak Mayer, had suggested that Israel's ministry of foreign affairs take over responsibility for the dormant accounts affair from the Jewish NGO's. The World Jewish Congress, the WJRO as well as the Jewish Agency violently rejected the proposal, accusing the ambassador of giving greater importance to reasons of State than to the defense of Jews. The World Jewish Congress also reminded that for many years it had had a mandate from the Israeli government to be in charge of such matters.[53]

Radicalism and intolerance of the World Jewish Congress

The policy the World Jewish Congress followed during the crisis can be described as pure activism. Its behavior was punctuated with a series of media-grabbing declarations, sizzling accusations and angry threats against Switzerland. The general impression such actions created was one of immoderation and a lack of intellectual honesty. But as much as the strategy was morally questionable, it was frightfully effective. It goes without saying that the World Jewish Congress is a well-organized interest group...willing to go to any lengths to achieve its aims!

The World Jewish Congress had a three-pronged strategy: concentrate on the weak link; claim the highest amount possible; and practice "double outflanking."

---

[53] See *Le Temps*, May 18, 1998.

The first prong comes down to the following: break the weakest link (in this case Switzerland); stand on this success to better attack other, stronger countries and to get the domino principle going. This explains why the World Jewish Congress singled out Switzerland for most of its attacks. To the World Jewish Congress, Switzerland seemed like the weakest country, the quickest to yield ground, and the likeliest to make large amounts of compensation available to Holocaust survivors or the heirs of victims. The World Jewish Congress could not have been more right. Switzerland's Achilles' heel, as we have seen, indeed is its isolation, its vulnerability and, especially, the vulnerability of its banks. Another important factor that favored singling out Switzerland is the fact that the light the country likes to project itself in does not always tally with its real track record.

Of course the World Jewish Congress never went public with this strategy. The admission of such a programed country-hunt would have hurt its own image. The World Jewish Congress leaders therefore always publicly affirmed that Switzerland was not the only country involved and that they were not singling the country out (they would say so, wouldn't they!). An example of such watch-my-lips-talk was offered at the World Jewish Congress executive council meeting held in Oslo, Norway, on October 25 and 26, 1996. There it was again clearly stated that apart from Switzerland, other countries too were or would be called into question, that no effort would be spared in casting light on the grimmest moments in European history. The other countries named were the Central and Eastern European countries, Norway, France, Belgium, Italy, Portugal, the United Kingdom and even the United States. Such talk was repeated time and time again, even at the London conference in December 1997, where the World Jewish Congress leaders repeatedly stated that Switzerland was only one of many countries standing accused.

But such talk changed not an iota of the ceaseless attacks in 1997 and the first half of 1998. Rolf Bloch, chairman of the Jewish Communities in Switzerland, also pointed this out in June 1997, warning against a continuation of attacks focusing exclusively on Switzerland.

The lack of criticism of the other countries compounded the impression that Switzerland was being singled out. Flagrant double standards were thus consistently applied, both by the World Jewish Congress and the other Jewish organizations, especially the Jewish Agency. While showing no mercy to Switzerland, criticizing it for not acting fast enough in response to Jewish demands, the organizations remained tight-lipped about countries *slower* than Switzerland. Edgar Bronfman, asked shortly before the London conference what his reaction was to the slow progress of the British investigation into assets confiscated from Jews in the war, replied that it was not to him that such questions had to be asked, but to his British friends! Thus, when countries other than Switzerland were discussed, the World Jewish Congress's standard approach was to walk on eggs. As pointed out before, up to May 1998 the United States itself took no initiative on the dormant accounts in American banks. This was strange indeed as a great number of these accounts could reasonably have been expected to belong to Holocaust victims or survivors. Up to that point though, the World Jewish Congress had never raised the issue in the U.S. As stated earlier on in this chapter, the World Jewish Congress has its headquarters in the United States; which makes it even more unusual that the World Jewish Congress has never sought to find out more about the post-wartime role American banks, especially the Federal Reserve, played in transactions involving gold stolen by the Nazis. There can be one conclusion only: double standards doubly over.

The World Jewish Congress also adhered to the second prong of its strategy (claim the highest amount possible) throughout the crisis. In its public statements the Congress stated that the moral and financial aspects were inseparable and had to be taken into account at the same time. But again the Congress' actions called the bluff of such verbal eye-wash. If mores weighed as much as money, why did the World Jewish Congress so shamelessly push the Swiss banks to agree to a quick deal involving enormous amounts of compensation while the banks have already set up a solidarity fund under which urgent financial aid was made available to any needy Holocaust survivor? Why, if truth weighed as much as treasure, did the World Jewish Congress not let Switzerland's transparent and rigorous search for dormant accounts and their subsequent restitution to the lawful owners, their heirs or, if neither could be found, to charities, take its course, allowing the full truth to come out? If mores and truth were what motivated the World Jewish Congress, it would have waited too for the publication of the findings of the historical commission Switzerland set up – with the Jewish organizations' explicit approval. Likewise, if the World Jewish Congress desired truth, it would have waited for a verdict in the class action suits in the U.S. True, a verdict would doubtlessly have taken years; and the plaintiffs might not have obtained satisfaction, or obtained the amounts they wished to get. But the truth would have been established. The World Jewish Congress, however, desired not truth but the maximum amount of compensation they could get away with. This explains their resorting to the most brutal methods available and pushing for a quick, global deal.

The third prong is a double "outflanking" in the World Jewish Congress strategy. On the one hand, during the crisis, this organization quickly sought to go beyond the dormant assets issue and to extend the debate to the issues of gold bought by Switzerland to Germany, trade relationships between Switzerland and the Third Reich, and Jewish refugees. The pressure on Switzerland was strengthened by linking or even consolidating these various issues to give as negative an image of Switzerland as possible. This strategy also allowed the World Jewish Congress not to be limited by the financial claims in the dormant assets issue, as it soon realized that hardly more than 80 to 100 million Swiss francs would be found on dormant accounts in Swiss banks. On the other hand, a second extension of the strategy was to involve not only private banks but also the Swiss Confederation and the Swiss National Bank. This aspect of the strategy was apparent in the attitude of the World Jewish Congress during the negotiations for a global agreement. The World Jewish Congress attempts were not successful as both the Confederation and the National Bank refused to get involved. But the strategy was financially efficient: in addition to the compensations related to dormant assets, the amount obtained under the global agreement and paid by the Swiss banks included the sums the World Jewish Congress claimed back from the Confederation and the National Bank for gold bought by Switzerland from Germany and the compensations for hardship owed to Jewish refugees who had been rejected by Switzerland during the war.

Against this updated strategy, we shall now turn to the methods used by the World Jewish Congress, which are functionally linked to the strategy adopted. Although they form a consistent whole serving the strategy of the organization, the methods can be classified, in our opinion, in seven categories.

Firstly, the World Jewish Congress devised against Switzerland a campaign that was orchestrated at the international level by using a highly efficient public relations machine. In this crisis Switzerland has been, as we have already shown, the target of a real smear campaign reminding us, as to the methods used, of the campaign the World Jewish Congress had carried out ten years earlier against former UN Secretary-General and Austrian President Kurt Waldheim. Of course the two affairs cannot be compared because they are substantially different and involve a state and its banks on the one hand and an individual on the other. Yet the methods used – a far-reaching and lengthy campaign – are similar in nature. Tom Séguev, an Israeli journalist, writes about the leaders of the World Jewish Congress: "Their war against Swiss banks is their latest far-reaching project, since their unfortunate attempt to prove that Kurt Waldheim was a war criminal."[54]

Secondly, the World Jewish Congress did not hesitate, throughout the crisis, to bring with unbelievable violence the most extreme and peremptory accusations against Switzerland, and was unable to give them any sound justification. This led some observers to speak of brutal and unacceptable attacks. Such was the dramatic announcement that Swiss banks were keeping billions of dollars in dormant accounts. After an investigation process unequaled in the world, we know now that the total amount of dormant accounts will be less than 100 million Swiss francs, including interest. Of course these sums should never have been in Swiss banks and this is not to the latter's credit. The difference between the two figures shows, however, the extent to which the World Jewish Congress accused Switzerland by issuing totally arbitrary figures. In its effort to blacken Switzerland and its banks, the World Jewish

[54] *Ha'aretz*, September 15, 1996. On the way the World Jewish Congress conducted its campaign against Kurt Waldheim at the international level, see an excellent study by a Belgian historian, Jean Vanwelkenhuyzen, "L'affaire Waldheim ou les pièges du refoulement" (The Waldheim affair or the traps of repression), *Revue générale*, no. 8-9, 1988, pp.11-39.

Congress forgot two basic truths: many assets that were supposed to be in Switzerland had been extorted out of their owners by the Nazis before they could be transferred out of Germany; and an important proportion of Jewish assets transferred in Switzerland either were only there in transit or were later transferred in other countries that seemed to offer greater security (U.S.A., U.K., Canada).

Another example of a World Jewish Congress peremptory accusation against Switzerland is related to gold stolen by the Nazis which ended up in Switzerland. At the London Conference in December 1997, World Jewish Congress leaders, on the basis of a report by historians their own organization had mandated, did not hesitate to assert that Switzerland kept nearly 3 billion dollars in Nazi gold after the war because 85% of the gold transferred out of Germany had transited through Switzerland. According to this report, the proportion of non monetary gold (i.e. gold stolen from individuals and companies) came up to 30% and not to 15% as believed so far. This increased in the same proportion the sums Switzerland should have reimbursed after the war.[55] Many observers and experts stressed that such assertions were disputable and immoderate but this did not prevent the accusations from contributing, through their impact on public opinion, to an increasing pressure on Switzerland by damaging the image of this country and of its banks.

Along the same lines, Bronfman, at a meeting of the Knesset Committee on the restitution of Jewish assets, declared that trains filled with Jews had gone through Switzerland on their way to the death camps, or that anti-Semitism was now

---

[55] *International Herald Tribune*, December 3, 1997.

growing in Switzerland at a faster pace than in any other country.[56]

Other dramatic statements by the World Jewish Congress illustrate the same type of methods. In particular, its president, Edgar Bronfman, accused Switzerland, in its role as Hitler's banker, of having prolonged the war for about two years. This kind of peremptory assertion pertains to irresponsibility or to intellectual dishonesty and is part of a tactic used by the leaders of the World Jewish Congress : to bring loud and extremely violent accusations to compel the other party to negotiate. This is what Edgar Bronfman acknowledges in his autobiography, *The Making of a Jew*,[57] when he describes the tactics successfully adopted to compel the Soviet power to authorize Jewish emigration. Perhaps the American Jews' hold over the World Jewish Congress is an explanation but in no way can it justify such brutal methods. When he became president of this organization in 1981, Bronfman boosted its action by using vindicatory or even brutal methods, which proved very efficient over time. They are in sharp contrast with the more discreet methods used by the World Jewish Congress when it was headquartered in Europe and most of its leaders were European Jews. Executive Director Elan Steinberg recalls that, "the World Jewish Congress has been kept as a confidential organization for a long time because discreet, behind the scene diplomacy was the rule after the war. Today, the time has come for an American-styled diplomacy – less shy, more aggressive, proud to defend Jewish interests."[58] Methods that are common in the United States were shocking for many European Jews who question today the legitimacy of using, when advocating a

---

[56] *Basler Zeitung*, November 26, 1997; *Neue Zürcher Zeitung*, November 26, 1997.

[57] *The Making of a Jew*, New York, G.P. Putnam's Sons, 1996.

[58] *New York Times*, February 16, 1997.

sacred cause, harsh methods that are sometimes dishonorable for those who use them.

The World Jewish Congress was not, however, the only organization to use methods made up of extremely serious, ungrounded global accusations. The Jewish Agency, in particular its president, Avraham Burg, adopted such methods on occasions. Similarly, the Simon Wiesenthal Center in Los Angeles used them with an incredibly greater doggedness than the other Jewish organizations, as shown by the two surveys published by this center on Switzerland's past.

The first survey, published in January 1998, deals with "forced labor camps" in Switzerland between 1940 and 1944.[59] Written by American historian Alan Morris Shom at the invitation of Marvin Hier, Dean of the Simon Wiesenthal Center, this report accuses Switzerland of having forced Jewish refugees to work like slaves in the worst of circumstances. According to Shom, the Swiss exhibited sadism toward the Jews. In a second survey submitted in June 1998,[60] Alan Shom declared that during the dark years, Switzerland was strongly anti-Semite and pro-Nazi. This attitude was supposedly characteristic of the working classes and the political and economic elite as well. In other words, the actions of Nazi and fascist groups influenced the Swiss society as a whole and determined a deep pro-Nazi feeling.

Both surveys elicited strong reactions in Switzerland because they were pernicious and deceptive, and lacked scientific rigor. Simon Wiesenthal himself – although the Los Angeles center bears his name, he has no responsibility in its management – did not agree with the two reports. By asserting that they brought dramatic and spectacular revelations, the Simon

---

[59] *The Unwanted Guests: Swiss Forced Labor Camps (1940-1944), op. cit.*
[60] *A Survey of Nazi and Pro-Nazi Groups in Switzerland: 1930-1945, op. cit.*

Wiesenthal Center succeeded in creating a media event widely echoed in the United States and damaging for the image of Switzerland in this country. By systematically trying to make the front-page news, the Center was also somewhat seeking to put a bid on relentlessness to position itself with regard to the World Jewish Congress in the global negotiations with Switzerland.

A third type of method used by the World Jewish Congress was to use unrelenting accusations against Switzerland as a basis for immoderate claims. Edgar Bronfman asked between 2 to 3 billion dollars to Switzerland at the London Conference in December 1997.[61] Another example is the requirement that Holocaust victims be explicitly mentioned amongst the beneficiaries of the future Swiss Solidarity Foundation. World Jewish Congress Vice-President Lord Greville warned that a possible omission would be "an unacceptable and fundamental failure in the confidence relationship." [62] Along the same lines, the Swiss bankers were required in March 1998 to reimburse not only the sums on dormant accounts that were actually discovered (which is perfectly right) but also to offer compensations to plaintiffs whose accounts are unknown or who can only prove that their assets were stolen by the Nazis. One might wonder then how really useful are the Volcker Committee and the systematic search for dormant accounts that was jointly agreed and organized by the Swiss Bankers' Association and the World Jewish Congress. Now let us remember that many assets only transited through Switzerland to end up in other countries, notably the United States and Britain. If this World Jewish Congress requirement had been followed, the Swiss banks would be now offering compensations to plaintiffs

[61] See in this connection the review published in *Neue Zürcher Zeitung*, December 3, 1997.

[62] *Tribune de Genève*, November 14, 1997.

whose assets (in fact, their parents' assets) were stolen by the Nazis and to other plaintiffs whose assets are now on dormant accounts in the United States or Great Britain after having transited through Switzerland before the war. We see how absurd this requirement was.

We should note, however, that even though the Swiss banks refused it, this requirement probably contributed through the pressure exerted to convincing them to accept a global agreement on a very important one-time payment (1.25 billion dollars); ultimately, this means that they paid *de facto* compensations to plaintiffs whose assets are not in Switzerland.

A fourth method frequently used by the World Jewish Congress is systematic and relentless criticism of the other party, whatever the latter may try to do. Immediately after the first Eizenstat report was issued, the Swiss government published a very moderate statement highlighting certain limitations in the report. The World Jewish Congress, through its vice-president Kalman Sultanic, declared that the statement was "disappointing and worrying," adding, "it shows a failure in facing the requirements of history and truth."[63]

The same systematic criticism was expressed after the Swiss Bankers' Association published the second list of dormant accounts in October 1997. This association had logically decided to exclude from the list some 63,000 accounts containing less than 100 Swiss francs (the average sum per account was 18 francs), declaring that the total amount of these accounts, i.e. 1.1 million francs, would be donated to the Swiss Red Cross for its Childhood Assistance Programs in Switzerland and abroad. The World Jewish Congress reacted harshly and did not acknowledge the Swiss banks' exemplary efforts although they were in line with the agreement the World Jewish

---

[63] *Nouveau Quotidien*, May 23, 1997.

Congress had reached with the Swiss Bankers' Association, and denounced these efforts as being a new deliberate dissimulation attempt on the part of Swiss banks.[64]

The same kind of violent and systematic criticism implying denigration of the other party is apparent in Edgar Bronfman's statements, e.g. his statement on Swiss leaders: "Money seems to be their creed. Anything they've got, they will hang on to at all costs."[65]

A fifth method the World Jewish Congress seems to have used with some success is amalgamation tactics: different files are closely associated by merging their claims. This is what happened with the dormant assets and the Nazi Gold issues and the World Jewish Congress consequently asked for a global settlement. The Swiss Confederation and the Swiss National Bank refused to get involved but the Swiss banks had to pay to meet all World Jewish Congress requirements – i.e. concerning Nazi Gold, refugees and dormant assets. Its leaders had clearly suggested that whoever paid, the compensations had to meet the requirements of all files.

The sixth method was a highly efficient use of political connections to support World Jewish Congress actions. Its president, Edgar Bronfman, is well introduced in political circles in the United States and other countries. His links with President Clinton allowed him to obtain that Stuart Eizenstat, a high-ranking diplomat, be entrusted with the file concerning Jewish assets stolen during World War II.

The tactical alliance with Senator D'Amato is the clearest illustration of this method. We feel that such an alliance was of a dubious nature and pertained to absolute cynicism. Bronfman was looking for an important American political

---

[64] *Nouveau Quotidien*, October 30, 1997.
[65] *Jewish Bulletin of Northern California*, March 1998.

middleman to support his actions against Switzerland. He contacted Senator Alfonse D'Amato, a very influential politician in New York State. The Senator was low in polls because of his repeated and unsuccessful attacks against Bill and Hilary Clinton in the context of the Whitewater scandal. Isabel Vincent writes: "Senator D'Amato, whose third term of office would end in two years, was looking for a cause that might help him secure his re-election. The cause Bronfman was proposing was providential, all the more so since D'Amato's constituency was largely made up of Jews. During the 1992 campaign for Congress, D'Amato had been supported by 40% only of Jewish voters, who represent about 10% of New York State voters. (...) D'Amato was clearly looking for a way of enhancing his public image before the next elections. Nazi Gold was the perfect issue to get his campaign started."[66]

This unclear alliance between an organization looking for a political middleman and a politician fishing for votes was a short-term success. By submitting the dormant assets issue to the Senate Banking Committee he chaired and by his relentless attacks against Switzerland, Senator D'Amato greatly increased the impact of World Jewish Congress claims. Now perhaps such actions based on cynical electoral calculations will, beyond their short-term success, be detrimental to the Jewish cause in the longer term. In the fall 1998 elections for Congress, New York Jewish voters refused to be cheated and to elect D'Amato for a new term of office and were followed by a majority of New York voters.

The seventh method was to exert on Switzerland the most extreme pressures, that were not far from blackmail. This is apparent in Edgar Bronfman's repeated threats against Swit-

---

[66] VINCENT, Isabel, *Hitler's Silent Partners: Swiss Banks, Nazi Gold, and the Pursuit of Justice*, Morrow, 1997.

zerland, especially when, feigning to ignore the actions achieved by Switzerland so far, he declared: "If the Swiss are going to keep digging their heels in, then I'll have to ask all the U.S. shareholders to suspend their dealings with the Swiss. It's coming to a point where it has to resolve itself or it has to be total war. I can't be sitting on my thumbs forever."[67] Similarly, World Jewish Congress Secretary-General Israel Singer gave his total support to Senator D'Amato's attempts to block a merger between Union Bank of Switzerland and Swiss Bank Corporation as long as Swiss banks did not meet the requirements of Jewish organizations. The World Jewish Congress used the same type of method when it strenuously attempted to convince various officials of American cities and States to take boycott measures against Switzerland if its major banks did not accept the requirements set by Bronfman and his organization. This was the conclusion reached by Sigi Feigel, Honorary President of the Zurich Israelite Community: "Today, (...) I can understand that people speak of blackmail. The boycott measures, the claims amounting to billions of dollars ... What do Americans have in mind? Their image of Switzerland is that of a country you only have to squeeze to get money out of it. This is sheer madness."[68] A Jewish American historian, Raul Hilberg, one of the best historians of the Holocaust in the world, did not hesitate to assert that "for the first time in history, the Jews have used a weapon that can only be termed blackmail. (...) I was totally upset by the rhetoric used by the World Jewish Congress. (...) There is no relation whatsoever between what the Swiss banks owed to Jews and what the World Jewish Congress required and obtained. I cannot find words

---

[67] *Jewish Bulletin of Northern California*, March 1998.

[68] *Le Temps*, April 15, 1998.

strong enough to say that the man who presides over the World Jewish Congress does not speak on my behalf."[69]

The illusions of the global settlement

This analysis of the methods of the World Jewish Congress necessarily entails a number of questions. Of course we are glad that fifty years after the Holocaust the survivors or descendants of victims of this terrible tragedy ask proudly for justice and reparation. But we wonder if, after a short-term material success, the arrogance, extravagance, cynicism and brutality so characteristic of such methods will really bring justice. For Michael Kohn, former President of the Swiss Federation of Israelite Communities, the question is: are such methods really legitimate or do they not dishonor those who use them?[70] In other words, if the mission the World Jewish Congress has set for itself is honorable, if it deserves respect and support, did it not miss the target by using means that seriously affected the Jewish cause? We feel that, for the leaders of this organization, the end justifies the means. It is possible to restore truth and justice by treading them under foot?

The World Jewish Congress, by its determined actions supported by other Jewish organizations and the initiators of U.S. class action suits, greatly contributed to reaching the August 12, 1998 agreement with the major Swiss banks. The 1.2 billion dollars global compensation obtained under this agreement was a success as it met almost all its requirements. In that sense, the agreement was undoubtedly a complete victory for this Jewish organization which had taken the lead in the campaign against Switzerland and had been the driving

[69] Interview with *Weltwoche*, January 28, 1999.
[70] Interview with *Tribune de Genève*, May 13, 1998.

force in the negotiations for a global agreement, and of course for the plaintiffs and the victims who obtained the compensations.

However, in view of the circumstances, perhaps this apparent victory is more of a moral defeat, a Pyrrhic victory indeed, and this for two reasons.

Firstly, as we have just noted, the moral cost of victory is likely to be high due to the methods used. Moreover, a noble and just cause might well have been ill-served by the fact that certain protagonists exploited the cause for their own political and electoral ambitions and that some organizations made it serve a quest for power that requires important financial resources.

Secondly, by basing their claims and the global negotiations on money and financial compensations, the World Jewish Congress and most international Jewish organizations overlooked the moral aspects of the whole affair. True, the leaders of the World Jewish Congress stressed that, in their opinion, material and moral aspects were closely related and that moral reparation had to materialize in material reparation. But the question is whether the choice of an approach based on deals and material compensations affected the moral imperatives, in particular the duty of remembrance. Is the financial agreement really global? Was it sufficient to close the file? We do hope that this is true at least at the material level. If not, the agreement would be a piece of deceit. Negotiations conducted by deals and the agreement obtained did not close the books on the moral level. How could we dare to think that an important financial compensation would be enough to make for the moral responsibility of Switzerland when it decided to drive back Jewish refugees, condemning them to extermination in the death camps? This is the reason why many Israeli circles felt so uneasy during the negotiations and when the global agreement was achieved. Controversy and material claims appeared to be a de-sacralization of the ethical issues related to the extermination of one third of the Jewish people. Many Israelis had profuse doubts about the deals that led to the global agreement.

The same question was raised by Michael Kohn, former President of the Swiss Federation of Israelite Communities: "An overwhelming majority of Swiss believe that the only thing Jews want is money. The attitude of the World Jewish Congress reconfirms their impression. Once the global agreement is signed, people will say, 'now that we have paid, don't bother us any more.' Such endless financial deals are causing a saturation in the Shoa issue. People are fed up. Money has replaced morality and ethics. The duty of remembrance and the research needed on Switzerland's past behavior are becoming secondary issues."[71]

We might fear that this priority of money over ethics and the methods used to obtain financial compensations contributed to strengthening anti-Semitism.[72] Now whatever the abuses of certain Jewish organizations during the crisis, in no way do they justify any form of anti-Semitism. As any form of racism, anti-Semitism must be absolutely opposed, for it is the negation of human dignity, it scorns what makes the greatness of human beings: tolerance and respect for others. It would be very sad indeed if this crisis, which should have given the Swiss, motivated by a moral imperative, an opportunity to have a critical look on their past, led some of them on the way to rejection and intolerance. This would be all the more unfortunate since the behavior of Swiss Jews was exemplary during a

---

[71] Interview with *Tribune de Genève*, May 13, 1998.

[72] About the risk of anti-Semitism growing in Switzerland in relation to this crisis, see the comments made by Gabriel Padon, the Israeli ambassador to Switzerland, in *Neue Zürcher Zeitung*, September 15, 1997.

crisis that was so distressing for them. While expressing their concern for justice and truth, they clearly opposed the abuses of the «American» Jewish organizations and their attempts at exploiting the past to gain maximum profit from it.[73]

[73] See a remarkable book by Françoise Buffat and Sylvie Cohen, *Suisses et juifs. Portraits et témoignages* (The Swiss and the Jews. Portraits and statements). Lausanne, Favre, 1998. The book adequately reflects the Swiss Jews' attitude during the crisis.

Chapter four

The ambiguous role of the United States

Throughout the crisis over dormant assets and Nazi Gold, the United States played a major role in a number of ways. First, the World Jewish Congress, an organization headquartered in the U.S. and where American Jews have a prominent influence, is a highly Americanized organization. The American authorities furthermore were directly and strongly involved at the federal level, especially with the Senate Banking Committee, the State Department, and the Under Secretary of Commerce Stuart Eizenstat, or at the level of the member States of the Union in the boycott announced against Switzerland and its banks. Finally, the American judiciary was chosen by American Jews for several class action suits against Swiss banks, an essential element in the process that led to a global agreement on August 12, 1998.

In the first instance, it is by considering the very particular position of the United States in the international system of today that we shall seek to shed light on its deep involvement in this crisis.

Imperial America

With the collapse of communist powers in central and Eastern Europe, the implosion of the Soviet empire and the close of the Cold War, the United States gained a position of total supremacy and exclusive hegemony. As the only superpower in the world, the American empire is the result not only of military supremacy but also of a decisive influence on the way commercial and technological networks are operated in an era of globalization. This American supremacy has been further strengthened by the good health of the economy, especially the exceptional growth the country has enjoyed since the mid-90s.

In view of this supremacy, the U.S.A. tended more than ever to dictate its law to the world, to consider its own criteria and standards as being universal, to rewrite history in its own way, to adopt international law to its own convenience and to consider that strength gives moral supremacy. Now this is no new phenomenon. The United States has always tended to exert legal imperialism, to have a foreign policy pervaded with a messianic attitude consisting of a reappropriation of ethics in order to assign immorality to others and to project American values as the standard for the entire world to follow, by feeling invested with a mission by Providence and by thinking that what is good for the United States of America is, by definition, good for the peace and prosperity of all. This propensity to dictate history, law or ethics is, however, stronger than ever today as a result of the supremacy that the U.S.A. enjoys. This was obvious during the crisis of dormant assets and Nazi Gold, when the United States, as the only world superpower at the end of the Twentieth Century and recalling its victory over Nazi Germany, felt justified in giving full rein to this natural propensity against a small isolated country, Switzerland.

Don't let us be naive, however: behind this messianic attitude lie powerful economic and political interests. The United States naturally seeks to keep a military, political and economic leadership over the world, to defend its own interests by relying on the law of might. This is apparent in the American policy toward Europe in the military field, with the concept of restructuring NATO and extending it to Eastern European countries and in economy and trade with its policy toward the European Union. However, we are bound to admit that the Europeans' weaknesses and dissension has favored this American unilateralism, as is shown by Europe's poor management of the Bosnian tragedy. Yet, we must never be led to forget that underlying the moral claims invoked by the United States lie the interests of an imperial power and that, as Secretary of State Madeleine Albright stated clearly, "one of the major objectives of our government is to ensure that it will be possible to extend the economic interests of the United States worldwide."[74]

Given these glaringly obvious facts that have nevertheless to be recalled, it is quite understandable that, in the crisis of dormant assets and Nazi Gold, many Swiss felt annoyed by the American propensity to rewrite history and to lay down the law, and felt that the United States was not in a very good position to give lessons of ethics. Jean-Luc Maurer pointed out that "what is rather shocking and even very irritating in this sad affair is that the moral lessons should come from a country which might well be the most powerful nation in the world, but is far from being the most virtuous and respectable. How could we fail to be scandalized by an almighty country which stands arrogantly as the universal moralist, while applying different and unequal standards to the others' faults as to its own. This hypocritical attitude doesn't greatly strengthen the legitimacy of a prosecutor whose stubbornness seems suspect."[75] Of course, this does not free Switzerland from undertaking a criti-

[74] *The Wall Street Journal*, January 21, 1997.

[75] *Journal de Genève*, June 23, 1997.

cal re-reading of its own past but has clearly to be kept in mind when we try, as we are doing, to make a close analysis of this crisis and the part the various actors may have played. We must understand that the competitiveness of the Swiss financial center for the American financial community is not unconnected to the U.S. behavior during the crisis. We have also to understand that the open opposition of American authorities to the Swiss bank secrecy in the name of transparency and of the eradication of money laundering played its part in influencing the behavior of the United States.

Drifts of a boycott

For the Swiss public opinion, the boycott measures decided by several member States of the Union and a number of American cities were probably the most obvious involvement of the United States in the crisis. Let us recall here that the whole affair began on October 9, 1997 when the City of New York announced sanctions against the Union Bank of Switzerland in the form of the exclusion of a group banking from an over 1 billion dollars loan issued by the City of New York. On this occasion, we learned that, without any prior public announcement, California had imposed a trade moratorium on the major Swiss banks suspending any new business with them as long as they had not demonstrated the most complete transparency in the settlement of the dormant assets matter. Soon after these events, other member States of the Union, starting with Massachusetts, publicized their intention of taking similar measures against Swiss banks. Waves of boycotts were looming on the horizon, all the more so since New York City's comptroller Alan Hevesi announced he would invite 800 representatives of the finance administration, pension funds and State-owned funds to a meeting on December 8 in New York. This meeting was to deal with the restitution by Swiss banks of dormant assets belonging to victims of the Holocaust. Senator D'Amato and the president of the World Jewish Congress were invited to address the conference.

The New York conference did not decide any immediate boycott action against Swiss banks, but chose to exert strong pressures by granting them a moratorium on sanctions until March 31, 1998, the deadline for a settlement of the dormant assets problem under a global agreement to be concluded with the World Jewish Congress and the lawyers representing the initiators of class actions against the Swiss banks. This agreement was also to cover the issue of gold stolen from Holocaust victims by the Nazis and bought by Switzerland. On March 26, 1998, a fresh conference decided to extend the moratorium for a further three months period while building pressure on the major Swiss banks in order to compel them to accept a global agreement.

When this new moratorium expired, several States and cities opted for sanctions against Switzerland, as the negotiations for a global agreement had come to no conclusion at the end of June 1998 after the negotiators had refused a 600 million dollars offer made by the Swiss banks.

Against this historical background, we have now to turn to the motivations of the various actors in this process. Their statements clearly express an intention to sanction Swiss banks for their guilty behavior, whether in the past with regard to Holocaust victims who held funds in Switzerland[76] or today

[76] For example, see the statement made by Bill Nelson, Director of the Florida insurance surveillance body: "We do not do business any longer with institutions – whether they are banks or insurance companies – that got rich on the back of the victims of the Holocaust."*Le Temps*, July 16, 1998.

because of an attitude deemed both arrogant and uncooperative (see for instance the Meili affair so often quoted in these types of arguments). However, other, deeper motives inspired the actors: a desire to bring to bear powerful pressure tactics, and electoral interests.

If a boycott of the Swiss banks might indeed have had important effects in the longer term, especially if it had been enforced by a growing number of States and cities, we have to admit that this threat and the resulting bad corporate image did exert a strong pressure on the major Swiss banks and contributed to a large extent to speeding up the global negotiations and driving them to a conclusion. This is what the Chicago representative, Burton Natarus, meant when he declared: "Every time Jewish people become too conciliatory, we loose out. We have to exert as much economic pressure as we possibly can, so that these people can have these assets returned to them."[77] Thus, the announcement of a boycott to be enforced in the long term was first of all an extraordinary pressure tactic, as illustrated by the three months extension of the moratorium deadline (March 31, 1998) decided on December 8, 1997. Additional evidence of this key role of boycott can be found in the fact that, on July 1, 1998, the committee chaired by Alan Hevesi simply decided to cancel the moratorium on sanctions, leaving each State and city free to decide on the desired action. In most cases, the sanctions were announced together with a few months enforcement time, a *de facto* extension of the moratorium.

This use of the boycott threat as an instrument of pressure is in perfect harmony with the threats and pressures wielded by the World Jewish Congress. Moreover, the leaders of this organization were very active in this process involving a pressure

---

[77] *The Inquirer Philadelphia*, March 15, 1998.

constantly rising based on a boycott threat: they attended meetings of the finance officials of local communities organized by Alan Hevesi and declared that they fully supported the sanctions. Significantly, at each stage in this process the representatives of American cities and States took decisions that were totally in line with the requests of the president of the World Jewish Congress.

Clearly, Switzerland was not the first country to be under heavy fire from U.S. States or cities. In the past, several countries, first of all South Africa in view of its apartheid policy, had been exposed to economic sanctions by American local communities. At the time when the moratorium concerning the major Swiss banks was canceled, no less than nine U.S. States and 23 cities were enforcing sanctions on various countries such as Burma, China, Nigeria and Cuba. The boycott measures inevitably irritated the federal government, which felt that it had the sole responsibility for U.S. foreign policy. This exasperation, also expressed by the State Department about the sanctions against Switzerland,[78] was not sufficient, however, to dissuade the American local communities from using these methods since they felt they were fully empowered to choose their investments and their financial partners.

Local and regional American public protagonists tend to use sanctions with great ease against foreign countries not only because they think sanctions are useful instruments of pressure but also, in a probably deeper and more decisive way, because they have electoral motives. In the crisis with Switzerland, it is easy to understand that elections gave the elected representatives good reasons not to disappoint Jewish voters and to hold

[78] See the joint statement of the American and Swiss governments (March 26, 1998) in which the calls for boycott measures are deemed unjustified and counter-productive.

to a firm line toward Switzerland by lining up on the demands of the World Jewish Congress. This was particularly true in the cities of States where the Jewish constituency is important, for instance in New York where Jewish voters account for about 10% of the voters.

One can well understand the American administration was annoyed that the member States of the Union and the local communities, by enforcing a policy of sanctions against several foreign countries, were interfering in the fields of U.S. foreign policy and trade under the responsibility of the Federal State. However, the American administration was not highly credible when, in objecting to sanctions against Switzerland, it argued that such measures were counterproductive: this same Administration uses sanctions, sometimes in an excessive way, to the point that they have now become a privileged foreign policy tool. In recent years, an inflation in the use of sanctions against foreign nations by the American government has been observed. From 1993 to 1996, sanctions were used 61 times against 35 countries, which accounts for more than half of the sanctions enforced since 1945. Seen thus, the behaviors of the local communities and of the federal government respectively can be considered as being in complete harmony.

This increasingly frequent and broader use of sanctions by the United States is a manifestation of a deviation and is a source of concern. Its most extreme expression lies in the U.S. adoption of extraterritorial acts, i.e. acts containing provisions aimed at a unilateral extension of American regulations to third-party countries, or even to the international community as a whole. This is what happened with the so-called Helms-Burton and D'Amato-Kennedy Acts which include extraterritorial aspects and were adopted on March 12, 1996 and August 5, 1996, respectively.[79]

The Helms-Burton Act, the "Cuban Liberty and Democratic Solidarity (LIBERTAD) Act", was adopted both to reinforce the embargo against Cuba and to respond to an openness of the Cuban government to foreign investors. This act forbids any individual to have commercial or financial activities related to former U.S. property which became government-controlled by the Castrist regime. It allows American citizens or companies, victims of this nationalization, to sue any individual or company whose business or financial activities are related to these assets in American courts. Moreover, admission in the United States may be denied to these persons or business executives.

The D'Amato-Kennedy Act, the "Iran and Libya Sanctions Act of 1996", is aimed at depriving Iran and Libya of the resources needed for developing their weapons industry and funding international terrorism. To this end, it applies sanctions to foreign companies investing more than 40 millions dollars yearly in the petroleum and gas industry in these two countries.

---

[79] For a detailed analysis of these acts and their extraterritorial nature, see: STERN, Brigitte, "Vers la mondialisation juridique? Les lois Helms-Burton et D'Amato-Kennedy" (Toward legal globalization? The Helms-Burton and D'Amato-Kennedy acts), *Revue générale de droit international*, no. 4, 1996, pp. 970-1003. See also: KRESS, Claus, HERBST, Jochen, "Der Helms-Burton-Act aus völkerrechtlicher Sicht", *Recht der Internationalen Wirtschaft*, vol. 43, no. 8, August 1997, pp. 630-641. REINISCH, August, "Widening the US Embargo Against Cuba Extraterritoriality: a Few Public International Law Comments on the Cuban Liberty and Democratic Solidarity (LIBERTAD) Act of 1996", *European Journal of International Law*, vol. 7, no. 4, 1996, pp. 545-562. See also: HUBER, Jürgen, "La réaction de l'Union européenne face aux lois américaines Helms-Burton et D'Amato" (How the European Union reacted to the Helms-Burton and D'Amato acts), *Revue du Marché commun et de l'Union européenne*, no. 408, May 1997, pp. 301-308.

These two acts raised much protest, especially in Europe, because their extraterritorial nature conflicts with international law and with the rules governing international trade. In view of a potential conflict with the European Union, the American administration sought to restrain the enforcement of these acts in spite of a very hostile Congress. Nevertheless, they express a legal imperialism reflecting an evident contempt of international law.

The adoption of acts with an extraterritorial outreach, as well as, more generally, the increasingly frequent application of sanctions by the federal government are also connected to electoral motives. For American congressmen, the fight against « terrorist » nations, at a time when the United States felt threatened by terrorism on its own territory, could only be beneficial in terms of votes. In this connection, the anti-Iranian activism of the American-Israeli Action Committee and the powerful electoral impact of the Jewish American lobby had some influence. In the same way, the adoption of the Helms-Burton Act only makes sense in view of the electoral impact of the Cuban American ethnic minority.

Through this frequent use of international sanctions and the extraterritorial projection of American laws, U.S. foreign policy grew gradually more fragmented in answer to various pressures of an electoral nature. We feel that, following the end of the Cold War and the disappearance of the major threat represented by the Soviet Union, U.S. foreign policy lost its consistency and broke up into dispersed actions to take account of the demands of various lobbies and internal policy interests.

Abuses of a pernicious system: Class action suits against Swiss banks

Through extensive media coverage, the boycott measures decided by some American local communities were probably the most effective means in drawing the attention of public opinion to the crisis. However, the involvement of the United States in this confrontation was not limited to threats of possible sanctions: the American judiciary was chosen as the arena for a clash between many American Jewish plaintiffs and the major Swiss banks.

Three class actions were filed by tens of thousands of American Jews against the three major Swiss banks (Union Bank of Switzerland, Swiss Bank Corporation, Crédit Suisse). They concerned Jewish dormant assets and the wartime behavior of major Swiss banks, accused of having laundered the profits of Nazi atrocities, of having deliberately accepted the profits of Nazi looting and forced labor and of having prevented any restitution of stolen assets. The first suit was filed in 1996 by two lawyers, Edward Fagan[80] and Robert Swift, on behalf of Gizella Weisshaus and several thousands other plaintiffs. It asked no less than 20 million dollars from the Swiss banking institutions to compensate for Jewish assets that had not been given back to their legitimate owners. The same year, two lawyers, Mel Weiss and Michael Hausfeld, on behalf of Jacob Friedman and other Jewish plaintiffs, filed a second suit supported by the Simon Wiesenthal Center. A third suit of a similar nature came in 1997 from an ultra-orthodox Jewish

[80] Note that Ed Fagan was also the initiator of a 2.56 billion dollars suit against the Union Bank of Switzerland on behalf of Christoph Meili, a night watcher who had been fired by this bank for having discovered and transmitted to Jewish organizations banking archives concerning the Nazi period the bank was about to destroy.

organization, the World Council of Orthodox Jewish Communities. As the three suits shared the same scope – i.e. dormant assets belonging to Holocaust victims – and were aimed at the same banks, the Federal Judge of the district of New York, Edward R. Korman, asked the lawyers to aggregate.

Two lawyers, Melvyn Weiss and Michael Hausfeld submitted a fourth class action in June 1998 to the Federal Judge of the district of Washington, on behalf of five Holocaust survivors. This suit was not aimed at the three major Swiss banks but at the Swiss National Bank, accused of having accepted and kept after the war gold stolen by the Nazis.

Of course, the banks questioned the jurisdiction of the American judiciary. The Swiss National Bank pointed out – rightfully – that, according to the Foreign Sovereign Immunities Act of 1976, bodies in foreign states could not be sued by individuals in American courts. As to the commercial banks, they stressed that this matter should be dealt with by the Swiss judiciary and not by the American judiciary.

It is not on the legal level, however, that the role played by class actions in the crisis is to be assessed. In fact, they were used as a pressure tactic to obtain as much money as possible from the Swiss banks. And this was only possible because the American judiciary is so peculiar in many respects. To begin with, this system works in a spirit of a legal imperialism. Taking little account of the sovereign law of other countries, this system deems that, for occurrence which took place in foreign countries and for which American citizens feel prejudiced, the normal course of action is to by-pass the judiciary of these nations and go directly to American courts.

Secondly, the evolution of the American judiciary is a source of concern because it is often used as a money-making machine, by an immoderate use, through civil proceedings, of legal protections set up for citizens, especially consumers and minorities. The compensations asked for and very often obtained tend to be loosely related to the original offense.

Finally, this perversion of the spirit of the American judiciary grows on a very favorable ground because it allows for class action suits. This form of collective claim (class action suit) is widespread in the United States and allows one of several members of a group to file a suit on behalf of the group. The system has several basic benefits: it enables any justiciable, whatever his or her financial resources, to support effortlessly the high costs of a legal process; it avoids any saturation of the judiciary resulting from a proliferation of trials related to the same case; it fosters a fair treatment of all offended persons. On the basis of these theoretical advantages, the American legislative authority reduced the requirements of the Code of civil law procedure related to class actions in 1996.

In actual fact, however, the American judiciary is far from enshrining the theoretical benefits of this type of procedure. American courts are overwhelmed by a growing number of class actions, as the advantages of the procedure, including its reduced cost, encourage frequent cases by citizens who are thus inclined to use the legal process more frequently and to refuse risk and personal liability.[81] Moreover, an ever-growing number of class actions entail an abusive, perverse use of this procedure by lawyers who are mainly out for money. By inducing their clients to file suits against companies together with extraordinary financial demands (often amounting to hundreds of millions or even billions of dollars), these lawyers try to induce the companies to accept an extrajudicial settlement. For these companies, the legal process may become lengthy, unmanageable and costly. Many of them finally ac-

[81] In this connection, see DERSHOWITZ, Alan M., *The Abuse Excuse*, New York, Little Brown, 1995.

cept a transaction, even at high cost, to avoid not only the high direct costs of the procedure but also adverse effects on the corporate image created when a lengthy and protracted legal process finds a broad echo in the media. Moreover, the outcome is full of uncertainties for the company, as the verdict is delivered by a jury of citizens and not by judges. A company found guilty is condemned to pay not only important financial compensations for damage to the plaintiffs, but also a high financial penalty. Many companies subjected to class actions are thus driven to accept an extrajudicial settlement. In this way, they do not pay huge compensations to plaintiffs because of a responsibility established judicially, but simply for purely economic reasons (i.e. to avoid the risk of having to pay much more). Undoubtedly, what we have here is an immoderate use or even a perversion of a system in which the meaning of justice is far from being clear.

In the light of these few remarks on the class action procedure, we gain a better understanding of the situation of the three major Swiss banks when the three suits were filed against them in the United States. These suits fit perfectly well into the perverse logic of the immoderate use of a legal process and they express the deviation of a legal system that encourages all possible excesses, starting with those of lawyers who are out for image building and big commissions.

The excessive amounts the Swiss banks were asked to pay (in the tens of billions of dollars), the time-consuming and costly legal process and its highly uncertain outcome, the necessity to submit innumerable documents to the judge and, consequently, to incur the risk of violating Swiss bank secrecy, prompted the banks to accept the idea of an extrajudicial settlement involving payment of very high compensations to plaintiffs. Thus, a global agreement was reached on August 12, 1998. This agreement undoubtedly represents a very fortunate outcome for the survivors of the Holocaust and for the descendants of victims of this ghastly tragedy, but it should be acknowledged that the process that led to the agreement was more a game of pressures and deals than a quest for justice.

When studying closely and in a critical way the process leading to this global agreement, we are really faced with pressures and deals, or rather with deals carried out under pressure. The three major Swiss banks, under the real threat of sanctions, were compelled to accept a final showdown. We understand better now that the outcome could only have been unfavorable to them. The suits as well as the potential consequences of the legal process exerted very strong pressures that were even more determining than the boycott measures decided by several American local communities. The use of a particular judicial procedure proved the most powerful tool to make the Swiss banks surrender. In that sense, we can say that this tool was fully part of the strategy of the World Jewish Congress, even if the interests of the initiators of these class actions were not exactly the same as those of the World Jewish Congress as an organization mainly seeking to reinforce it legitimacy and power.

Everything concurred to bring about a quick extrajudicial settlement, provided that it was of a global nature and would protect the Swiss banks against any future action. When the World Jewish Restitution Organization announced in July 1998 a further class action to come against the major Swiss banks and the Swiss National Bank, the pressure for such an extrajudicial agreement became stronger.

Senator D'Amato's opportunism

Senator Alphonse D'Amato was undoubtedly a leading actor in the crisis of dormant assets and Nazi Gold. He was one the staunchest accusers of Switzerland and of its wartime behavior as well as of the Swiss bankers' management of assets entrusted to them by Jews who eventually became Holocaust victims.

As Chairman of the Senate Banking Committee, he was in the best possible position to give high visibility to his attacks against Switzerland, as well as to initiate and conduct investigation and public debate procedures, which largely contributed to the growing pressure on Switzerland and its banks. This Banking Committee almost became a self-proclaimed court by convening both the defendants and the plaintiffs and by pronouncing judgments. Relying on the weight of the United States as a country, Senator D'Amato even succeeded, by summoning representatives of Switzerland to the Committee hearings, in conveying the depressing image of a country compelled to explain itself to an American governmental body.

In the innumerable statements he made throughout the crisis, Senator D'Amato always portrayed himself as the staunchest defender of the Jewish victims of the Holocaust and their descendants, and spent all his efforts on seeking a legal outcome by forcing Switzerland, and especially its banks, to restore the victims' assets and to offer them compensations for hardship.

However, powerful electoral interests obviously underlie his dedication to the Jewish cause and his proclaimed love for justice. As pointed out in the preceding chapter, two simple facts must be taken into account: the importance of Jewish voters in New York (about 10% of voters); and the uncertainties surrounding Alfonse D'Amato's own electoral situation when he decided to put forward the interests of Holocaust victims. The senator, who was then under violent criticism for affairs he had been involved in and whom many voters accused of having wasted public money in his campaign against President Clinton in the Whitewater scandal, could see heavy clouds looming on his political future.

In 1996, when Alfonse D'Amato met Edgar Bronfman, President of the World Jewish Congress, and when the latter asked him to get involved in the question of dormant assets, he quickly saw the electoral benefits he could reap from the effort. A close association between Senator D'Amato and the World Jewish Congress came into being and it proved true and constant throughout the crisis. In the implementation of the strategy of the World Jewish Congress, Alfonse D'Amato was an essential political middleman.

D'Amato's commitment to the Jewish cause had one other advantage. It would be a natural supposition to imagine that, through his determined actions against Swiss banks, Senator D'Amato – while trying to secure New York Jewish votes – was making his friends in Wall Street not too unhappy to see Switzerland, a rival financial center, in an uncomfortable position.

Senator D'Amato's transparent electoral aims shed some doubt as to his explicit motivations for embracing the Jewish cause; from it emerges the portrait of a pure political opportunism. Such purposes clearly explain a biased behavior that cannot claim to exhibit a calm quest for justice but a deliberate intention to accuse Switzerland at all costs, by condemning the country in advance and refusing to acknowledge its efforts to solve the problems.

It seems all the more justified to question Senator D'Amato's real motives in this crisis if we consider that a troubled or even bad reputation had been hanging over his head for some years. On a number of occasions, Mr. D'Amato was brought into question for the links he might have had with members of several Mafia "families," on behalf of whom he was brought into contact with the judicial authorities. Moreover, according to the American press, including the *Wall Street Journal*, D'Amato supposedly received important electoral funds from Wall Street brokers. He turned down any close investigation of the Milken corporation in relation to the now famous "junk bonds" scandal by the Senate Banking Committee he chaired. Finally, in 1991, the Senate Ethics Committee blamed him for "inappropriate" behavior.

The doubts that one can harbor on the profound motivation of the senator's commitment to his political causes are strengthened when we review closely the methods he used in the crisis on dormant assets and Nazi gold. Senator D'Amato's actions and statements during the crisis do not reflect a genuine concern for seriously establishing the truth, but an intent to confuse things and draw attention on himself even by using very dubious means.

In an effort to discredit his opponents, Senator D'Amato frequently used arbitrary criticism stemming from pure bad faith. For instance, when the Swiss Bankers' Association published a second list of dormant accounts in October 1997, he declared, in a letter addressed to George Krayer, the president of this association, that "the Swiss banking system has lost its credibility", and declared "ridiculous" the fact that the banks were now publishing 4,000 names of dormant accounts holders after reporting earlier only a small number of accounts. In doing so, the New York Senator forgot to mention the exemplary measures taken by the Swiss banks in this investigation and to note that if the accounts amounted to 70 million Swiss francs, i.e. a lower amount than previously reported by them, they were far from reaching the 4-5 billion dollars claimed as the true amount by Senator D'Amato and several leaders of the World Jewish Congress.

As if arbitrary and hypocritical attacks were not enough, Senator D'Amato did not hesitate to voice insulting and vulgar accusations against his opponents. Reacting to statements made by Swiss President Jean-Pascal Delamuraz, who said that pressures on Switzerland and its banks were sheer blackmail, the senator answered that "the real blackmail occurred fifty years ago when Swiss bankers helped the Gestapo extort account numbers from persecuted Jews."[82] And to add insult to injury, concerning the reactions in Switzerland to the night watcher Christoph Meili affair, he warned: "The Swiss government must end this campaign of intimidation and coercion."[83] D'Amato went a step further in vulgarity and insult when he declared: "The facts will show clearly that the Swiss were involved in the greatest robbery in the history of mankind. The Swiss took billions of dollars in gold from the defenseless and the poor, and participated in this ugly killing machine to actually hide and launder assets, and to facilitate a war which caused the deaths of so many innocent people. For the Swiss government to suggest that they have no obligation to reopen the case and to look at the records is absolutely unacceptable. They should be ashamed of themselves."[84] The senator went even further in his immoderate rhetoric when he declared that "The world has already rendered its verdict: The Swiss were guilty. We're now debating the penalty, and the penalty should fit the crime."[85]

In a more subtle manner, Alfonso D'Amato makes frequent use of attacks on people's imputed intentions. For instance, he accused the commission responsible for the identification of dormant accounts, presided by Paul Volcker, former

---

[82] "Holocaust Assets and Swiss Banks", Senator D'Amato's web page.
[83] *Ibid.*
[84] "D'Amato statement on Swiss Financial Involvement with Nazis", U.S. Senator D'Amato, News Release, June 1, 1998.
[85] D'Amato statement, February 26, 1997.

President of the American Central Bank, of having as its sole rationale and goal to delay this investigation after fifty years of hopes and expectations.[86] Similarly, the New York senator questioned the seriousness and the viability of the Bergier Commission by asserting that it was preposterous to hear Jean-François Bergier, its chairman, declare that the work of this group of historians would last five years instead of the two or three years initially anticipated. Moreover, in Senator D'Amato's view, there was a conflict of interest due to the fact that Jean-François Bergier was a member of a cultural foundation established by the Union Bank of Switzerland.[87] D'Amato omitted to say that this foundation was totally independent from the bank and that Jean-François Bergier had already announced that he would retire from this foundation.

One of D'Amato's favorite methods was constantly to publicize his moves by flooding the Swiss and American fax machines with messages of dramatic revelations based on unpublished documents. After study, almost all the unpublished documents proved to be well-known cases, and the senator's "revelations" were rehashed stories of the past or even worse, biased interpretations based on an extrapolation of historical documents from their context.

His search for striking effects even on occasions prompted Senator D'Amato to make statements supported by no evidence, without taking the trouble to check the information. This was the case when he announced that the Swiss ambassador to Washington Jagmetti had virtually called for a war against Jews.[88]

---

[86] *Neue Zürcher Zeitung*, December 17, 1996.

[87] Prepared statement of Senator Alfonse M. D'Amato before the House Banking Committee Hearing on Swiss Banks, June 25, 1997.

[88] In this connection, see *Neue Zürcher Zeitung*, February 11, 1997.

Stuart Eizenstat: An emblematic ambiguity

The United States Under Secretary of Commerce, Stuart Eizenstat, is, with Senator Alfonse D'Amato, the American official who played the most important role in this crisis of dormant assets and Nazi gold. It was he that was entrusted to handle the file within the American administration. Under his authority, two reports of the American government were drafted and published. They bear his name and he wrote the foreword of both reports. Moreover, he became, in spring 1998, the "facilitator" in the negotiations between the major Swiss banks and the World Jewish Congress and the lawyers representing the initiators of class actions, a process which led to the global agreement reached on August 12, 1998.

Obviously, Eizenstat is a very different personality from D'Amato. He has the reputation of a serious and even austere man, a subtle diplomat who is very moderate in his statements and behavior. However, ambiguity best characterizes his attitude throughout the crisis. His behavior with regard to Switzerland was based on a subtle mix of firm pressure and sympathetic understanding. On the one hand, contrary to Senator D'Amato, who always accused Switzerland of doing nothing, the Under Secretary of State recognized the importance and the quality of Switzerland's efforts to solve the dormant assets problem and to bring full light on its past behavior. On the other hand, Stuart Eizenstat did not hesitate to make several value judgments on Switzerland, as the foreword to his first report shows clearly,[89] and to exert a permanent pressure on this country throughout the process.

---

[89] *U.S. and Allied Efforts to Recover and Restore Gold and other Assets Stolen or Hidden by Germany During World War II, op.cit.*

Thus, when the representatives of American local communities met in New York in December 1997 to discuss, at Alan Hevesi's invitation, possible sanctions against Switzerland, Stuart Eizenstat clearly declared that "Switzerland had undertaken a thorough and courageous effort to face its past earnestly and to discuss these matters openly. (...) The Swiss have acted a lot without being given the credit they deserve: To impose sanctions on them would really be inappropriate."[90] Yet, a few days earlier, at the London Conference on Nazi gold, he had declared that Switzerland could do more, without clarifying the nature of such efforts. Similarly, Stuart Eizenstat has always been ambiguous with regard to his position and his government's stance on a possible renegotiation of the 1946 Washington Agreement, leaving some doubt about the whole matter.

When the World Jewish Congress proposed a global agreement to Switzerland on December 1, 1997 covering a minimum one million dollar sum, Stuart Eizenstat declared: "I believe this is totally counter-productive and only helps to heat up the debate. We shall not settle the matter by increasing pressure."[91] This did not prevent him from acting with great determination as a "facilitator" in the negotiation process that resulted in the payment of 1.25 billion dollars by the major Swiss banks.

It is probably in his role as a "facilitator" in the negotiations for a global settlement that Eizenstat was mostly ambiguous. While being openly opposed to sanctions against Swiss banks, he used deftly the threat of sanctions announced by the representatives of local communities (American cities and States) to "suggest" to the Swiss Confederation to get involved with the Swiss banks in a global settlement, in view of the re-

[90] *Tribune de Genève*, December 9, 1997.

[91] *Le Nouveau Quotidien*, December 3, 1997.

port of the Bergier Commission on Nazi gold,[92] but he did not want to say if, in his opinion, this involvement was to be of a financial nature. The Swiss member of Parliament, François Lachat, Chairman of the Foreign Affairs Commission of the Swiss National Council (Parliament), pointed to this ambiguity when he said : "Stuart Eizenstat's attitude is ambiguous. He says he is opposed to sanctions but at the same time he asks the National Bank to participate in a global agreement. This is placing pressure on Switzerland, with the Clinton administration playing the good guy and the City of New York as the bad girl."[93]

Stuart Eizenstat's ambiguous attitude is emblematic in reflecting the general attitude of the representatives of the Clinton administration involved in the crisis, first among them Secretary of State Madeleine Albright and the American ambassador to Switzerland, Madeleine Kunin. Throughout the crisis, Ambassador Kunin, as well as Madeleine Albright in Bern on November 15, 1997, spoke with a subtle mix of ambivalent if not downright contradictory language. She praised Switzerland for its efforts and celebrated the American-Swiss friendship, but distilled some friendly bits of "advice" to induce the banks and the Swiss authorities to accept the requirements of the Jewish organizations without waiting for the conclusions of the work of the Volcker and Bergier commissions.

This ambiguous attitude of the American administration representatives and especially Stuart Eizenstat is probably largely instrumental in nature. It shows great intelligence and diplomatic skill. Underlying an often conciliatory tone and a cooperative attitude were brutal pressure and barely concealed threats. For instance, when the representatives of several

---

92 See *The New York Times*, July 12, 1998.

93 *L'Hebdo*, July 9, 1998.

American cities and States decided to cancel the moratorium on sanctions against the Swiss banks following the stalemate in the negotiations for a global agreement, Stuart Eizenstat sent out the following message: "The American government shouldn't tell Switzerland what to do, but it is time for this country to say how it will proceed to close this file in a conciliatory spirit." The Under Secretary of State, while still condemning sanctions in principle, was clearly telling Switzerland that it should abide by the requirements of the World Jewish Congress and of the initiators of class actions. Under the threat of sanctions, to demonstrate a spirit of conciliation could only be interpreted as an obligation to comply.

Beyond its tactical and instrumental aspect, this ambiguity probably stems from a tension between two kinds of interest. On the one hand, it was in the interest of the Clinton administration to avoid any trouble in its very good relationship with Switzerland, an important economic partner. Moreover, this administration had no interest in getting involved in a risky operation such as renegotiating the Washington Agreement, which could ultimately give rise to other revisions that might be potentially dangerous for the United States. On the other hand, the Democratic Party enjoys close links to the American Jewish community, one of its main donators. In view of the year 2000 presidential elections, this party, and especially Vice-President Al Gore, has no interest in alienating the Jewish lobby. As to Stuart Eizenstat, he has personal links with the Jewish circles and has been a member of the board of a number of Jewish organizations, including the very important American Jewish Committee. His *de facto* solidarity with the World Jewish Congress is clearly apparent in his action, including his involvement as a "facilitator" in the negotiations process which led to the global agreement in August 1998.

Of course, we cannot criticize Stuart Eizenstat for sympathizing with the cause advocated by the Jewish organizations, an attitude based on a highly respectable ethical commitment. However, by using brutal and often dishonest methods, these organizations have dishonored the cause they claimed to defend. Stuart Eizenstat does not seem to have grasped this aspect of things or perhaps he was not able to draw the full consequences. This deficiency was already apparent in the highly disputable foreword he wrote for the first report bearing his name. The text lacks rigor, contains arbitrary judgments not based on the content of the report, never takes into account the economic and political context of World War II, and reflects, over and above the "imperial" attitude of the United States, a deliberate intention to blacken Switzerland's past behavior in order to exert a strong pressure on Swiss business and political leaders. This shows that the Under Secretary of State was motivated by interests that led him, at least in these circumstances, to adopt an attitude that did not correspond to the image of intellectual rigor he tried to give of himself.

Chapter five

A duty of remembrance

The unrelenting attacks against Switzerland throughout the dormant assets and Nazi gold crisis, the abuses and the brutal, dishonorable methods of the World Jewish Congress and some American politicians gradually started to irk Swiss public opinion, including some parties within Switzerland's Jewish community. A growing feeling of disgust appeared in the face of systematic denigration and threats of sanctions against the Swiss economy. In Swiss newspapers, the readers' letters reflected this feeling well. An ever-growing number of Swiss became convinced that some people were trying to get as much money as possible from their country, even by using methods resembling blackmail. As one of the prominent members of the Swiss Jewish community, Sigi Feigel, said, "the fact that the term blackmail is used to qualify the American requirements is quite understandable. To act in this way against a sovereign state in which – and this has yet again to be hammered home – the Holocaust did not occur, is unacceptable. It seems that the latest rage in the U.S. is to treat Switzerland as some kind of supplier of billions of dollars."[94]

A growing feeling of exasperation in a widespread spectrum of political circles echoed this irritation of the Swiss pub-

[94] *Tages-Anzeiger*, April 3, 1998.

lic opinion. The president of the Swiss Radical Party, Franz Steinegger, declared that, in his opinion, Senator D'Amato's pressures were no better than the Nazis' own methods.[95] A Christian Democrat member of Parliament, Rose-Marie Siemen, member of the National Council (Parliament) Foreign Policy Committee, said that the Swiss could not let people insult them and use practices unworthy of civilized nations.[96] This exasperation was clearly apparent when the Foreign Policy Committee met a delegation of the World Jewish Congress led by Israel Singer. The Secretary General of this organization had to face severe reproaches from the Swiss members of Parliament, who required the World Jewish Congress to apologize for statements made by its president, Edgar Bronfman, who had threatened Switzerland with total war. The tension rose one degree higher in July 1998, after a stalemate in the negotiations for a global agreement and the decision taken by the representatives of several American cities and States to cancel the moratorium on sanctions against Switzerland. Thomas Borer, head of the Swiss Task Force, accused New York City comptroller Alan Hevesi of manipulating and disseminating false information. He added that this was an intimidation tactic reminding us of the most patent methods of propaganda. Thomas Borer was referring to an interview in the July 8 issue of the Swiss weekly *Weltwoche*, in which Alan Hevesi had criticized with the utmost violence the Swiss government and accused Thomas Borer of having deceitfully promised that the Swiss Confederation would participate in any eventual global agreement. Moreover, on July 22, with the undoubted support of the Swiss public opinion, Swiss President Flavio Cotti went

---

[95] *Le Nouveau Quotidien*, August 4, 1997.
[96] *Ibid.*

direct to the American President to take strong exception to the measures decided in the United States against Switzerland.

When a global agreement was reached on August 12, 1998 between the major Swiss banks and the Jewish organizations and the initiators of U.S. class actions, the violent pressure put on Switzerland ended. This agreement undoubtedly brought relief and peace to the Swiss public opinion, but as the World Jewish Congress and the plaintiffs had obtained a high amount of money, at the same time it strengthened the feeling that in the whole affair, money was more important than the quest for truth or ethics.

This feeling has certainly not been mitigated when the final results of the identification of dormant assets conducted under the auspices of the Volcker Committee have been published. While indicating that "there is confirmed evidence of questionable and deceitful actions by some individual banks in the handling of accounts of victims, including withholding of information from Holocaust victims or their heirs about their accounts, inappropriate closing of accounts, failure to keep adequate records, many cases of insensitivity to the efforts of victims to claim dormant or closed accounts, and a general lack of diligence – even active resistence – in response to earlier private and official inquiries about dormant accounts"[97], the Volcker report stresses that "the auditors have reported no evidence of systematic destruction of records of victim accounts, organized discrimination against the accounts of victims of Nazi persecution, or concerted efforts to divert the funds of victims of Nazi persecution to improper purposes".[98] Moreover, the audit carried out under the auspices of the Vol-

[97] Independent Committee of Eminent Persons. *Report on Dormant Accounts of Victims of Nazi Persecution in Swiss Banks*. December 1999, p. 13.

[98] *Ibid.*

cker Committee identified only a very limited number of dormant accounts probably or possibly related to Holocaust victims that were not included in the lists published by the Swiss banks in 1997. The aggregate value of the newly identified accounts and the published accounts amounts to about 75 million Swiss francs. The Volcker report clearly indicates that "on the basis on information now available, no valid estimate can be made of the aggregate value of the accounts due victims of Nazi persecution or their heirs until a claims resolution process has determined which claimants are properly entitled to such accounts".[99] However, we may deem that about 15% of the aggregate value of the dormant accounts found in Switzerland, i.e. 11 to 12 million francs, belonged to Jewish victims of the Holocaust. Part of these 11 to 12 million francs in dormant accounts held by Jews includes the accumulated interests to the present day. As for the remaining part, after a restoration of fees and charges by a multiplication of the implied 1945 book value by a factor of 10 to reach an adjusted current value, the final amount should not exceed 90 million Swiss francs. There seems to be good evidence that the total amount of dormant assets belonging to Jews, *including interest* will not exceed 100 million Swiss francs. We are far from the 5 to 7 billion dollars claimed by the World Jewish Congress and Senator D'Amato. When comparing the less than 100 million francs with the 1.8 billion francs paid by the major Swiss banks under the global agreement (almost a 1 to 20 ratio), many Swiss will indeed feel increasingly irritated.

This irritation is going to keep growing when the Swiss remember that the leaders of the World Jewish Congress declared that the 1.8 billion francs paid by the Swiss banks is justified by the fact that the 100 million francs found in Swiss

[99] *Ibid.*, p. 11.

banks would, after adding the interests, come to nearly 1 billion francs.[100] In doing so, these officials amalgamate in an unacceptable way the 15% (i.e. 11 to 12 million francs) of dormant accounts found in Switzerland and belonging to Jews, and the remaining 85% belonging to persons with no relation whatsoever to the Holocaust and its victims. Following the publication of the report of the Volcker Committee in December1999, several media made the same kind of amalgamation. For instance, the Washington Post conjured up the purely imaginary figure of 700 million dollars.[101] Even though the Volcker Committee recommended that a further list including about 25,000 accounts that might have some connection with Holocaust victims be published, we should note that most of these are not dormant accounts, but closed accounts. There was no justification for including such accounts in the list published by the Swiss banks.

Although this irritation and exasperation are perfectly understandable, it would be unfortunate if they were to induce the Swiss to refuse the required effort of memory. They should not take all these excesses as an opportunity to refuse to revisit their past in a spirit of reappropriation, by fully taking on the darkest pages of their history. This duty of memory, which is not restricted to Switzerland but concerns all those who played a part in the tragedy which gave birth to the Monster of the Holocaust, is an obligation today, for the end of the Cold War years has created the right conditions for a self-scrutiny of our past. Since the end of World War II, under

---

[100] See for example the surprising statements made by the Secretary General of the World Jewish Congress, Elan Steinberg, in an interview published by *Le Temps* on September 10, 1998. Taking as a basis the 100 million francs discovered and adding interest, Elan Steinberg gives an amount of 1 billion Swiss francs for bank accounts only.

[101] *The Washington Post*, December 13, 1999.

pressure from the priority requirements imposed by the East-West conflict, a process of selective memory has tended for decades to conceal some basically well known or easily accessible facts.

The Swiss must proceed with this effort of memory first and foremost for themselves, and not specifically for others. Their future lies in their ability to fully meet their past after challenging the image official Switzerland wished to cultivate. It would be a serious mistake to think that the financial provisions of the August 1998 global agreement free the Swiss from a moral obligation to remember; if this were the case, the World Jewish Congress would have paved the way for an attitude that focuses more on the financial aspects of the problem than on the moral aspects.

Similarly, it would be very unfortunate for the Swiss to think that they are discharged from any critical approach to their past because their country has no direct responsibility in the Holocaust and may have behaved better than many other countries during the dark years. As former Swiss State Secretary Franz Blankart wrote, "other nations fed the Jewish victims' wealth into their state-held funds, were more determined in refusing to grant asylum to Jewish refugees (Evian Conference, Saint-Louis ship), or continue to keep their houses under receivership. All this is obviously unfair, but does not liberate us from self-scrutiny, which should not in turn lead to legal concessions. This self-scrutiny must clarify truth, whether truth is good or bad to contemplate."[102]

However, it would be unfair not to recognize the efforts already made by Switzerland in reassessing its past and compensating for its misconduct. A remarkable job has been accomplished: the agreement between the Swiss Bankers' Asso-

---

[102] *Le Temps*, April 15, 1998.

ciation and the World Jewish Congress for finding dormant assets, the creation of the Volcker and Bergier commissions, the setting up of a special Fund with 265 million francs for immediate humanitarian help. True, these measures were taken only under external pressure and this is not to Switzerland's credit, in particular concerning the problem of dormant assets. This problem should and could have been solved long ago but the major Swiss banks, wrapped up in their narrow legalism, forgot that bank secrecy was intended to protect the clients of banks and not the banks themselves. However, it remains true that no other country has undertaken such wide-ranging actions as those decided by Switzerland during this crisis. The leaders of the World Jewish Congress and Senator D'Amato were not willing to recognize this fact because they found themselves embroiled in their own ambitions and tactical calculations.

These efforts must be pursued to their bitter end, without any concession. Beyond any reparation for injury, it is first and foremost important that each Swiss national be in a position to look at his or her country without complacency, overcoming on the one hand any systematic depreciation while not allowing the forming of the all-too-perfect picture of an exceptional and self-satisfied country on the other. In other words, this clear and honest look at the past should allow the Swiss to avoid any complacent concealment of the past, but without driving them either to desperate self-flogging. However, a reassessment of the past is a risky endeavor; according to the interests at stake at any given moment in time, any political trend or group could be tempted to exploit it.

We do not intend to proceed with such a reassessment in this chapter. Our goal is simply to suggest what is, in our opinion, at the very core of this process and to highlight a few elements to be taken into account in this new reading of the past.

Dormant assets: The lessons to learn

Over a fifty-year period since World War II, between 1945 and 1995, the Swiss banks undoubtedly refused to undertake any systematic identification of dormant accounts held by Holocaust victims. The narrow legalistic formalism of some banks even led them to oppose requests filed by the victims' heirs. Rainer Gut, President of the Board of the Crédit Suisse Group, clearly recognized this fact when he said: "The Swiss banks made deep mistakes. We had – and still have – to recognize the fact. In the past, we have demonstrated little compassion for the problems raised by dormant accounts. (...) By their cramped legalism and stubbornness, the bank officials did not heed the Holocaust victims' requests. The anger of the dispossessed grew stronger and is quite understandable."[103]

When the passions raised by this crisis are eventually quelled, we shall probably understand that, although the criticism against this unacceptable behavior of the Swiss banks was absolutely justified, the focus on Switzerland alone, often depicted as a country of cheats and crooks, was far less justified. The other major Western financial centers probably did not do better. The Geneva lawyer Michel Halpérin writes with justification: "Even Great Britain and the United States, the lesson-givers of today, acted essentially like Switzerland. Funds deposited in their banks by German, Polish and Romanian victims (most of them Jewish) of Nazism were sometimes seized as 'enemy assets'. Then, Great Britain used these Jewish assets to the benefit of British creditors who had not been paid by German, Polish or Romanian debtors! When by chance the as-

[103] A presentation at the "Dolder meeting" in Zurich in January 1999.

sets had not been confiscated, it took years of efforts and the same types of documents (death certificates, inheritance certificates, statements of accounts, (...) to recover them, and the British and Americans made no effort for their clients in this respect."[104]

Obviously, despite this rather bleak overall context, the Swiss banks are left with an obligation to recognize their wrongdoing and to meet their responsibilities by offering compensations when this is still possible. In this connection, the Swiss banks are not all in the same position. Some bankers, in particular private bankers, have been much more respectful of their clients' rights and undertook long ago to identify dormant accounts. The major banks have undoubtedly to bear the brunt of responsibility for the situation due to their attitude during these fifty years, especially within the Swiss Bankers' Association, an apex association in which they have a prominent influence. Soon after the end of World War II, it was through this association and in an effort orchestrated by the major banks, that the process allowing for a systematic identification of dormant accounts was blocked.

To claim, as some observers tend to do now, that the Swiss banks did absolutely nothing to identify dormant accounts or look for their holders because they sought mere profit and grew rich on the back of the victims of Nazism and their heirs, is both stupid and unfair. Such a reasoning stems from pure fantasy or absolute bad faith. This is also true of the statements to the effect that the dormant assets kept in Swiss banks run into the tens of billions of dollars. At the end of 1945, the total assets deposited in Swiss banks by clients from the Axis powers or occupied countries amounted to 734 million Swiss francs. As noted above, we know today that the total dormant assets

[104] *Tribune de Genève*, April 23, 1998.

now kept in Swiss banks amount to less than 100 million francs, of which only about 15 % belonged to Jewish victims of the Holocaust. Obviously, the Swiss banks could not have built their wealth on these few millions, even though we must acknowledge that the sums are important to the legitimate owners of the assets, who are often elderly persons, some of them in needy circumstances.

One of the reasons for this lack of any systematic identification of dormant accounts by the Swiss banks lies in the fact that the majority of the accounts, in particular those associated with Holocaust victims, contained only very small amounts of money, which made investigation costs prohibitive. However, the basic reason for the Swiss banks to hamper any systematic investigation of dormant accounts belonging to Holocaust victims in the post-war years is a simple, albeit saddening and even somewhat revolting, reason. As already noted in Chapter 2, absolute bank secrecy had led to an undiscerning and arrogant legalism and formalism, which neglected the most basic human duties. This practice lasted fifty years[105] and is based on a deviation from a *per se* respectable principle. We should not forget that bank secrecy had very positive effects for the majority of those persecuted during the Nazi era who transferred their assets in Switzerland: thanks to bank secrecy, these assets were protected. We should not question therefore the principle of bank secrecy itself, but its implementation. In a world where individuals can see that government power impinges increasingly on private life, the fact that a majority of Swiss people keep their faith in bank secrecy is understandable. However, by making this principle into an absolute rule,

[105] This aspect was acknowledged by Lukas Mühlemann, CEO of the Crédit Suisse Group. See *Journal de Genève*, December 6-7, 1997.

the Swiss banks have distorted it and forgotten that bank secrecy was intended to serve the clients, not the banks.[106]

In the face of such a deviation from the original principle, the Swiss political authorities were guilty of reprehensible weakness. It is true that the Federal authorities approached the banks on several occasions to ask for a systematic identification of dormant accounts. The Ministry of Foreign Affairs made a first request to the Swiss Bankers' Association in 1947. Under pressure from the Western Allies and the Jewish organizations, and pursuant to a secret clause of the 1946 Washington Agreement between Switzerland and the victors of the Third Reich,[107] the Federal authorities asked this association to carry out an enquiry among its members to identify the dormant assets belonging to victims of fascism. The bankers blankly refused, and the Swiss political authorities dropped the issue.

For the next fifteen years and despite new requests and pressures, the Swiss Bankers' Association stood by its absolute refusal to carry out any systematic identification of dormant accounts, while claiming that the assets found in Swiss banks only amounted to a few hundred thousand francs. Following various international pressures, only in 1962 did the Swiss government decide to overcome this Association's opposition and to adopt a federal decree imposing the identification and publication of "assets in Switzerland belonging to foreigners or stateless persons who had been persecuted for racial, religious

[106] See Daniel Guggenheim's remarks in "Ce qui n'a pas fonctionné chez les banques dans l'affaire des biens en déshérence" (What did not work in the dormant assets issue), *La Suisse face à l'Empire américain, op. cit.*, p. 232.

[107] This secret clause provided that the Swiss government should take "necessary measures to make available to the three Allied governments (United States, Great Britain, France), for assistance purposes, the amount of assets in Switzerland of victims of violence recently perpetrated by the former German government who are deceased without any heir."

or political reasons." When the decree was enforced, slightly more than nine million francs were recovered and were either given back to their legitimate owners or donated to humanitarian organizations when the owners could not be identified.

Here again, the political authorities showed great weakness since they did not make the necessary arrangements to ensure that the investigation would be systematic and comprehensive. We learned subsequently that this had not been the case, since about 15% of the 75 million francs discovered towards the end of the '90s belonged to victims of the Holocaust. In September 1997, a parliamentary Commission asked the managers of the three major Swiss banks and the president of the Swiss Bankers' Association to explain the "unacceptable and unqualifiable" way their banks implemented the Federal decree of December 20, 1962 on dormant assets. The terms "unacceptable" and "unqualifiable" used by the Swiss members of Parliament are fully justified; they should apply, however, not only to the bankers' conduct but also to the careless and lenient attitude of the political authorities of the times.

We had to wait for the beginning of the crisis in 1996 to see the Swiss Bankers' Association come to grips with the problem of dormant assets and try to find a decisive solution under the lead of its president Georges Krayer, a thoroughly rigorous person, deeply concerned with justice. When the list of names associated with dormant accounts was published in July 1997, Georges Krayer did not hesitate to declare publicly that the attitude of the banks made him feel ashamed. "I am ashamed. When I read the 1,872 names on the list that we issue worldwide, I realized that it had never been very difficult to find the heirs. We shall never find a veil wide enough to hide the neglectfulness of my post-war colleagues."[108] However, the president's task was still difficult because several banks, which were members of the Association, dragged their feet by using dilatory methods, as they were unwilling to challenge in a radical way a policy applied since the end of World War II.

Was Swiss neutrality immoral?

Besides the criticism on the dormant assets belonging to Holocaust victims, the most serious reproach addressed to Switzerland during this crisis was probably that related to its policy with regard to Nazi Germany. It was argued that this policy had been characterized by an active and in-depth collaboration that went well beyond the requirements of neutrality. Neutrality could in fact have been merely a lure and a cover used to disguise serious compromising activities of a doubtful nature with the Third Reich, through behavior dictated largely by a Swiss economic and political elite acting out of self-interest.

Some observers were thus led to assert that the major question should be to ask why Switzerland went beyond the simple state-to-state collaboration needed for survival and, in a political attitude not without some zeal, did more than was necessary.[109]

To raise the issue in these terms, however, is both questionable and dangerous since an unacceptable bias is thereby introduced into the analysis. Before investigating the motives

---

[108] *Le Nouveau Quotidien*, July 24, 1997. Along the same lines, see also the highly critical stance taken by Heinrich Schneider, one of the leaders of the Swiss Bankers' Association, in the *Neue Zürcher Zeitung*, January 27, 1997.
[109] See for example the discussion organized by the German television ZDF on July 13, 1997 after the film *Nazi Gold*.

that led Switzerland to actively do more than was needed, we should try first to determine if this country really did more than the survival required. In other words, did Switzerland really and systematically use its status as a neutral country to obtain immoderate economic and financial benefits?

The first Eizenstat report, and more precisely the foreword written by the Under Secretary of Commerce himself, seems to give a clear answer. According to Eizenstat, Switzerland did misuse its neutrality, just as other neutral countries did. "The Swiss were the principal bankers and financial brokers for the Nazis (...)."[110] For the American Under Secretary of Commerce, "if self-defense and fear were factors in that rationale for neutrality, so too were profit in all neutral countries and outright Nazi sympathy in some. (...) Whatever their motivation, the fact that they pursued vigorous trade with the Third Reich had the clear effect of supporting and prolonging Nazi Germany's capacity to wage war."[111]

Moreover, according to Stuart Eizenstat, "of all the neutral nations, the one with the most complex roles in World War II, together with the deepest and most crucial relationship with Nazi Germany, was Switzerland. Switzerland's role was very mixed. It ended World War II as one of the wealthiest nations in Europe."[112]

Finally, Stuart Eizenstat feels that neutrality during World War II has to be considered an immoral practice because this war was so peculiar in nature. "In the unique circumstances of World War II, neutrality collided with morality; too often being neutral provided a pretext for avoiding moral considerations. Historically a well-established principle in international law, neutrality served for centuries of European wars as a legitimate

---

[110] *Eizenstat Report, op. cit.*, p. IV.
[111] *Ibid.*, p. VIII.
[112] *Ibid.*, p. X.

means by which smaller nations preserved their political sovereignty and economic viability. But it is painfully clear that Argentina, Portugal, Spain, Sweden, Switzerland, Turkey and other neutral countries were slow to recognize and acknowledge that this was not just another war. Most never did. Nazi Germany was a mortal threat to Western civilization itself, and had it been victorious, to the survival of even the neutral countries themselves."[113]

The leaders of the World Jewish Congress and of other Jewish organizations as well as Senator D'Amato took up Stuart Eizenstat's assessment to criticize harshly Switzerland for its neutral policy during the war. For instance, the Secretary-General of the World Jewish Congress, Israel Singer, in a lecture delivered at the University of Saint-Gall on January 21, 1998, declared that "neutrality is almost as bad as open collaboration."[114]

To this American criticism of Swiss neutrality during the war, one might be tempted to answer that the United States is not in the best position to criticize Switzerland's conduct. Not only did the United States strongly contribute to the economic and military build-up of Nazi Germany by their investments in this country until 1939, but they did not react, from 1935 to 1938, to Hitler's repeated violations of the Versailles Treaty and of international law. Moreover, it remained neutral until the Japanese launched their attack on Pearl Harbor on December 7, 1941. Such arguments have some justification. It is impossible to understand and assess the American attitude with regard to Swiss neutrality unless we see that it is perfectly in line with the messianic, dualistic, moralizing and even hypocritical and cynical logic, which underlies the rhetoric and the

---

[113] *Ibid.*, p. VII.

[114] *Le Nouveau Quotidien*, January 22, 1998.

international demeanor of the American superpower. In our opinion, however, it is not at this level that the matter should be discussed: to highlight the flaws in the American conduct is of no help in assessing Swiss neutrality during World War II. Swiss neutrality must be assessed on its own grounds and by considering Switzerland's situation in the wartime international environment.

The first element of this assessment is related to the particular nature of World War II. Did Nazi Germany's racist and expansionist ideology justify, as Stuart Eizenstat seems to believe, a change in Switzerland's neutrality and in the rules governing international public law? In other words, was this war so different from others that any application of neutrality would be doomed to be immoral? Two answers were given to this essential question. For the Americans, World War II was not a war like any other war. It was fundamentally different in that its objectives were not to fight against a mere enemy but against a criminal regime which endangered the fundamental values of democratic societies and embodied absolute evil. Given the nature of the enemy, neutrality was inconceivable and became immoral. For the Swiss, on the contrary, whatever the specificity of the conflict, only one principle was applicable: the permanent neutrality to which Switzerland is subjected is an obligation of international law based on several centuries of practice, recognized and imposed by the Treaty of Vienna in 1815 and declared to be in the interest of peace by the signatories of the Treaty of Versailles in 1919. This permanent neutrality applies to any conflict.

We have here widely diverging interpretations on the nature of neutrality. While in Switzerland the traditional conception of permanent neutrality was adhered to and, in contrast to occasional neutrality, imposed permanent requirements on the neutral nation, in the United States neutrality was considered simply an instrument that could be adapted according to circumstances. In that sense, the United States did not really distinguish between permanent neutrality and occasional neutrality.

This American view of neutrality associated with the U.S. tendency to make any conflict and their stakes absolute inevitably led this country to misunderstand and challenge Swiss neutrality. This position was not only expressed during World War II, but also during the Cold War when the United States tended to portray the Soviet regime as representing absolute evil, as they had done before with the Nazi regime. From the American viewpoint, the East-West conflict was also of a peculiar nature in that it opposed the forces of liberty and democracy with the forces of totalitarianism and evil. In the face of this recurrent American attitude, we have the right to ask on what grounds can a country, whatever its power, decide to set itself up as the only judge to decide when the specific nature of a conflict allows it to overrule international law and, in that specific case, to judge the status of permanent neutrality enjoyed by some nations.

From these few considerations, we can see that the American stance on neutrality is far from being convincing. Underlying its often hypocritical moralistic stance are the interests of a superpower, and the American position bears the seeds of a form of relativism which might seriously endanger the major principles of international public law.

A second useful element for an assessment of Swiss neutrality is related to Switzerland's situation in its wartime international environment. Even if we acknowledge the particular nature of the conflict, as liberty and democratic values had to be preserved from the assaults of a fascist totalitarianism, we must ask whether Switzerland could have defended these values better by abandoning its neutrality and declaring war on Germany instead of staying neutral.

In our opinion, the answer to this question is clear and is not disputable: if Switzerland had given up neutrality and had declared war on Germany, in no way would this have helped to preserve liberty and democratic values. On the contrary, Germany would have quickly invaded the country and the unique island of liberty and democracy in the heart of Europe would have disappeared. One should not forget Switzerland's very specific geographical situation during the war: a small isolated country, surrounded by the Axis forces and with no support from the Allies. As the latter would have been unable (at least until the end of 1944) to help a country invaded by Nazi Germany, Switzerland could only have hoped to preserve its independence, territorial integrity and democratic system by staying neutral, even at the cost of a few concessions. It has to be recalled, in Jean-Pierre Ritter's words, that "the primary duty of a state is to ensure the well-being of its nationals and consequently it cannot be criticized for any endeavor to this end, provided that it does not violate its own obligations. This maxim governs international relations today as it did in the past and the United States strictly complies by it."[115]

As to whether Switzerland should have given up neutrality in the course of the last months of the war, the answer can only be no, because if such a decision had been taken, this nation would have been rightfully accused of being merely opportunist.

We must add that if Switzerland had been invaded by Germany, the fate of the 10,000 Swiss Jews, of the 10,000 foreign Jews living in Switzerland and of the some 20,000 Jewish refugees in Switzerland would have been tragically sealed. Would the zealous opponents who criticize Swiss neutrality

[115] *Journal de Genève*, May 28, 1997.

during the war in the name of ethical values have wished to see this? Unless one adheres strictly to an ethics which places conviction as the sole value and takes no account of the consequences of the application of moral principles ("*fiat justitia pereat mundus*"), one cannot be unaware of the tragedy that would have resulted for the Jews living in Switzerland from an invasion of the country by Hitler's forces.

Moreover, by preserving its territorial integrity, Switzerland undoubtedly eased the Allies' task during the liberation of the continent. For Swiss historian Antoine Fleury, "Switzerland's greatest merit and its most important contribution to the victory over the Axis countries lies in the fact that the Allies were not obliged to invest men and resources to free this Alpine country if it had been occupied as all the other central and eastern European nations had been, and then to feed and reconstruct it."[116]

Finally, by staying neutral, Switzerland could play the very useful role of a protective power for nearly half of the countries in the international system. Its role was especially useful in defending prisoners of war.

In the light of these few elements of an assessment, we can see the extent to which Stuart Eizenstat's hasty assertions and non-historical value judgments are disputable. As many observers have already pointed out,[117] the text of the Eizenstat report written by American historians led by William Slany in

---

[116] Mr. Antoine Fleury at the hearings of the Committee on Banking and Financial Services (U.S. House of Representatives) chaired by James A. Leach, Washington DC, June 25, 1995.

[117] For example, see KREIS, Georg, "A la recherche d'une image historique 'correcte'. Interrogations à propos d'une récente tentantive d'interprétation" (In search of an 'adequate' historical representation. Some questions raised by a recent interpretation), in Yves Fricker *et al.*, *La Suisse face à l'Empire Americain. L'or, le Reich et l'argent des victimes* (Switzerland and the American Empire. Gold, the Reich and the victims' money), Geneva, Georg, 1997, pp. 240, ss.

no way supports the sharp judgments made by Stuart Eizenstat in the foreword.

However, there remains one question: in applying its neutrality during this tragic period, did Switzerland make too many concessions and go beyond what was needed to maintain its existence as a sovereign state? From what we know today, it seems that this was true at times, as was tragically shown by some aspects of the Swiss policy with regard to Jewish refugees, to which we shall come back later. Similarly, Swiss companies and citizens probably benefited unduly and ignominiously from the relationships Switzerland had to maintain as a neutral nation with Germany. Yet, while condemning such cases of inexcusable behavior with the utmost vigor we must be careful not to judge Switzerland's conduct without taking into account the historical context in its entirety, including Switzerland's isolation within Europe, which had been totally conquered by the Axis forces. In this difficult situation, it was almost impossible for Switzerland to define the limits of the economic concessions to the Third Reich that it had to make in any precise way in order to preserve the country from German invasion.

The difficult issue of Nazi Gold

Gold trading between Switzerland and Nazi Germany during World War II is at the heart of a deep controversy over how the Helvetic Confederation made use of its neutrality during these dark years. In a proportion of almost 4 to 5, the Reichbank's gold transfers abroad either ended up in Swiss financial institutions or were there in transit. The total amount of German gold bought by Switzerland stands at 1.6-1.7 billion francs, 13% of which transited through Swiss commercial banks and 87% through the Swiss National Bank. Transactions by Swiss commercial banks were all completed before October 1941; from then on, the central Bank was the only bank to receive German gold.

At the Conference on Nazi Gold convened in London in December 1997, Switzerland's transactions in gold with Germany were strongly criticized and, of course, they form the basis of one of the reproaches made to Switzerland by Jewish organizations and American plaintiffs throughout the crisis. The Bergier Commission interim report on gold, issued in May 1998, also contributed to criticism of Switzerland on the subject of these transactions.

This issue was much talked about in the media and the international public opinion for gold has a high symbolic significance – gold often raises powerful cravings and baseless fantasies. This is what happened with the so-called Nazi Gold. Indeed, during this crisis, a totally false image started to get around: supposedly this Nazi Gold transferred from Germany to Switzerland during the war had been stolen by German leaders and secretly placed in Swiss banks which kept it without the right and now refused to give it back. The recurrent myth of the Nazis' hidden treasury resurfaced yet again.

However, the facts do not correspond to this fiction that was complacently fed by some not too serious or deceitful media. The so-called Nazi Gold was in fact gold transferred from Germany (from the German central bank) to Switzerland by the Third Reich authorities and either bought by the Swiss National Bank (and also, until October 1941, by some Swiss commercial banks) or only in transit in Switzerland, acting as a clearing house. Therefore, this gold had nothing to do with the booty that some Nazi leaders might have individually collected and transferred out of Germany in a safe place. This gold exported by the German Central Bank does raise a serious problem, however, because the Reichbank incorporated to its own reserves – and therefore into the gold transferred abroad – the gold reserves seized in the central banks of the occupied countries, as well as gold stolen from individuals, including Jews who were victims of the Holocaust. In addition to this question as to the dubious origin of gold sold by Germany to Switzerland, we must ask whether Switzerland, by doing business in gold with Germany, helped to support the economy of the Third Reich and therefore to prolong the war.

Before bringing some elements of an answer to these questions, we need first to study the ends to which these transactions were put, then place the Swiss purchase of gold from Germany within the wider framework of Swiss transactions in gold with foreign countries (including Allied countries), and lastly take into account the motivations underlying the decision of the Swiss National Bank to enter in such transactions.

According to the Bergier Commission interim report,[118] out of a total amount of gold worth 1.6 to 1.7 billion francs delivered by the Reichbank to Switzerland during the war, the Swiss National Bank bought gold worth 1.2 billion Swiss francs. The remaining sum was entered in deposits which other central banks and the Bank for International Settlements had in Bern. A huge proportion of the gold purchased by the Swiss National Bank was resold to third-party countries, including Portugal (452 million francs), Spain (185 million francs) and Romania (102 million francs).[119] By selling gold to the Swiss National Bank, Germany could secure the Swiss francs needed to pay for raw materials bought from third-party countries. We must understand that, except for a few leasing or barter transactions, two principal means were available to Germany during

[118] *Switzerland and Gold Transactions in the Second World War. Interim report, op. Cit.*, p. 191.
[119] *Ibid.*

the war to pay for products purchased from European third countries: gold or the Swiss franc, the only effectively convertible currency during this period. With Swiss francs obtained for the raw materials exported to Germany, the central banks of third countries bought back a least part of the gold that the Swiss National Bank had previously purchased from the Reichbank. These triangular operations also took the following form: Switzerland paid for gold purchased from Germany in escudos bought from Portugal, which enabled Germany to pay Portugal in escudos for raw materials.

Thus, the transactions in gold allowed Germany to buy tungsten, zinc and food products from Portugal, manganese and agricultural products from Spain, chrome from Turkey and iron ore from Sweden. Some of these raw materials were probably important for Nazi Germany, in particular the tungsten and chrome needed by the weapons industry. Yet, it should be acknowledged that the most important raw materials needed by Germany – first among them petroleum products – were not obtained through gold sales to Switzerland, because the Reich procured them either through its allies (Romania) or from occupied nations (the occupied regions of the USSR). To assert that transactions in gold between Switzerland and Germany were absolutely vital for the Reich and that their effect was to prolong the war is therefore somewhat excessive.

Moreover, these Swiss purchases of gold from Germany must be set within the wider framework of all the transactions in gold carried out by Switzerland during the war. The Swiss National Bank did not only buy gold from Germany, but also from the Allies, in big amounts. According to the Bergier Commission interim report,[120] from 1939 to 1945, Switzerland purchased gold worth more than 2.2 billion francs from the

[120] *Op.cit.*, pp. 135 ff.

United States, more than half of which can be traced to a capital flow from the United States (mainly in 1940) leading to a conversion of dollars into gold.

The motives of the Swiss National Bank in operating these important transactions in gold with Germany and Allied countries were probably manifold, but the main one was certainly related to the application of the monetary policy laid down for the Swiss central bank. In the "gold standard" system of the 30s and 40s, the National Bank was responsible for maintaining the stability of the Swiss franc by ensuring gold parity. The purchase of gold abroad was the main tool of intervention used by the Swiss National Bank to maintain gold backing and to ensure monetary stability in a situation characterized by a growing demand for Swiss francs. During the war, this task was not easy at all, since the National Bank had to maintain the convertibility of the franc, the only means available for a sustained confidence in the Swiss currency. Monetary stability allowed Switzerland to continue purchasing abroad the raw materials necessary for its survival, and undoubtedly contributed to the program aiming at a reinforcement of the national defense capacities. However, the requirements of gold backing to which the Swiss National Bank was subjected during World War II must be put into perspective: on May 17, 1940, a secret decree edicted by the Swiss government discharged the National Bank of this obligation.[121]

Another motive put forward by the senior executives of the Swiss National Bank is that the important transactions in gold were intended to dissuade the German Reich from invading Switzerland. By becoming indispensable as the only European financial center with the only truly convertible currency and by allowing Germany to buy Swiss francs to pay for

[121] See Ibid., p. 140.

some of its imported goods, Switzerland thought it could divert the German leaders from their invasion projects and that the status of a neutral country anyway required a non-discriminatory attitude toward any third-party country.

Moreover, the Bergier interim report indicates that "after Swiss assets in the U.S. were frozen on 14 June 1941, the SNB – and later the Confederation – was no longer able to control its currency reserves freely, despite the fact that these reserves had been legally obtained and that title to their ownership was not disputed."[122] Blocking them froze the assets of individuals and drastically reduced the right to use gold that the Swiss National Bank had deposited in Western Allied countries. This financial blockage decided by the Allies in violation of The Hague Convention of 1907 posed serious problems to the Swiss National Bank as it concerned nearly 2.3 billion francs, a very high sum representing nearly two thirds of Switzerland's total monetary reserves.

Obviously, there was no profit-seeking in the motivations of the Swiss National Bank for conducting its transactions in gold with Germany. According to its own statistics, profits from reselling gold bought from the Reichbank amounted at that time to 18.4 million francs. It is on the basis of this amount that the Swiss National Bank senior executives decided to contribute 100 million francs to the solidarity foundation created in 1997, an amount corresponding in present value to the 18 million francs of the war years.

The central problem raised by these wartime transactions between Switzerland and Germany is related to the origin of the gold sold by the Reichbank to the Swiss National Bank. We know that the Reichbank incorporated in its reserves during the war gold seized in the central banks of several occupied

---

[122] *Op. cit.*, p. 135.

countries, mainly Belgium and The Netherlands; according to estimates of the Bergier Commission interim report,[123] these foreign reserves amounted to 483 million dollars. In addition, German gold included gold worth 82 million dollars, which had been stolen by the Nazis from individuals; of this amount, 2.9 million had been stolen from the victims of concentration camps ("Melmer gold").[124] These facts elicited strong criticism against Switzerland, especially from the World Jewish Congress.

Concerning gold seized by Germany from the central banks of conquered countries, a final answer is not easy to give. From the viewpoint of international public law, this question elicits diverging answers and interpretations.[125] However, it has no concrete implications nowadays since the Washington Agreement concluded in 1946 by Switzerland and the Allies solved it. Under this agreement, Switzerland agreed to a payment in gold worth 250 million Swiss francs as a contribution "to the pacification and reconstruction of Europe, including supplies for devastated countries," whereas the Allies relinquished «any claim against the Swiss government or the Swiss National Bank concerning gold bought from Germany by Switzerland during the war."[126]

Yet, we must wonder if the policy followed by the Swiss National Bank was politically and morally sound. This raises

---

[123] *Ibid.*, p. 39

[124] *Ibid.*

[125] See in particular VAGTS, Detlev F., *"Switzerland, International Law and World War II", The American Journal of International Law*, vol. 91, no. 3, 1997, pp. 466-475. RITTER, Jean-Pierre, "Or et biens en déshérence au regard des traités et du droit" (Gold and dormant assets with respect to treatises and law), *Journal de Genève*, January 6-7, 1997; THURER, Daniel, "Raubgold und Völkerrecht: eine Analyse im Lichte der Haager Landkriegsordnung", *Neue Zürcher Zeitung*, February 20, 1997.

[126] The Washington Agreement of May 25 1946, Diplomatische Dokumente der Schweiz, vol. 16, (1945-1947), Zürich, Chronos Verlag, 1997.

of course the question of good faith on the part of this bank. According to the Bergier Commission interim report, there is no doubt that its senior executives were aware of the dubious origin of gold bought to Germany, which did not prevent them, in a «business as usual» attitude, from pursuing their transactions in gold with the Third Reich. For the Bergier Commission, their arguments to justify their transactions with Germany – viz. the requirements of a monetary policy aiming at maintaining the stability and convertibility of the franc, the intention of discouraging Germany from invading Switzerland, the obligation of a neutral country not to discriminate among countries at war – are not convincing and were a posteriori justifications of the policy adopted for the purchase of gold.

Although we must clearly recognize that this policy of the Swiss National Bank raises highly complex issues, particularly on the moral level, it is impossible, in our opinion, simply to discard these arguments as non-convincing, as the Bergier Commission does in its interim report. This attitude resembles a dubious a priori moral judgment, itself stemming from a viewpoint very remote from the imperatives which should guide a historian's work, as it overlooks the economic and political context just to emphasize current requirements. As already pointed out above, our judgment on the actors' motivations and behaviors cannot be based on our current knowledge and criteria. In doing so, we would be ignoring the economic and political context of the past and, above all, the actors' own perception of affairs. We might consider today, in the light of our present knowledge, that this perception was biased or even false, but it was not ungrounded given the circumstances that prevailed at that time. For instance, in their intention to discourage Germany from invading Switzerland, perhaps the Swiss authorities accepted compromises which look excessive to us today but they cannot be absolutely condemned in view of the actors' wartime situation. In particular, we must recognize how difficult it was for them to define the limits beyond which the refusal of certain compromises with Germany would have impaired Switzerland's policy of deterrence. It may be difficult to assess how really important deterrence was in the gold transactions policy conducted by the Swiss National Bank with the Reichbank. The fact that the senior executives of the Swiss central bank gave this motive in 1943 serves only to raise some doubts as to its true importance, but this should not suffice to believe, with the authors of the Bergier Commission interim report, that "this argument was an a posteriori justification of the policy applied in matters of gold." Between having doubts and making such a peremptory judgment, there is a wide gap, which should not be crossed so easily. This assertion should not prevent us from regretting, as the Swiss government did when the Bergier interim report was published, that the senior executives in question did not demonstrate a higher moral and political awareness.

Gold stolen by the Nazis from the victims of the Holocaust is a totally different problem. This gold was incorporated in the Reichbank reserves and then sold to Switzerland. On this aspect, the conclusions of the interim report of the Bergier Commission are clear: "The total value of the gold shipped by the Reichsbank to Switzerland which is known to have been stolen from the victims of Nazi oppression is SFr. 581,899. Although the subject of gold confiscated from Jewish deportees was discussed by the SNB management in late 1943, there is no indication that those responsible for deciding SNB policy were aware of the origin of such gold shipped by the Reichsbank to Switzerland."[127] While recognizing the drama

[127] *Switzerland and Gold Transactions in the Second World War, op. cit.*, p. 191.

and pathos of the fact that gold stolen by the Nazis from the victims of the Holocaust was included in German sales to Switzerland, one should nevertheless observe that these 120 kg of gold (worth 581,899 Swiss francs) represent only 0.04 % of the total gold bought by Switzerland to Germany, and this does not fit the image given today of Switzerland as a greedy country, trying to get rich to the disadvantage of the victims of the Holocaust.

The distressing problem of refugees

The problem of refugees is undoubtedly the most distressing problem Switzerland has to face today in remembering and reassessing the past. Material assets are not at stake here as in the issues of dormant accounts and transactions on gold, but the very life of persons threatened by the Nazis' folly and hate on the grounds of race or religion. What did Switzerland, a neutral nation with a long humanitarian tradition, do to protect and save persons who were risking annihilation by the most horrible destruction machine ever devised by man? How did this country respond to these desperate human beings who knocked at the door to ask for help and shelter?

Alas the answer is tragic. We know today that at least 24,000 Jewish refugees were taken back to the Swiss border and that most of them ended up in Nazi death camps.[128] Moreover, by asking Germany in 1938 to include the distinctive "J" stamp in the passports of German Jews, Switzerland proved regrettably zealous and helped to tighten the net in which these persons were caught. The figures are clear and Switzerland's responsibility is undeniable, as recognized by

[128] Independent Commission of Experts Switzerland - Second World War, *Switzerland and Refugees in the Nazi Era*, Bern, December 1999.

Swiss President Kaspar Villiger in 1995, when the 50th anniversary of the end of World War II was commemorated.

Without relativizing in any way Switzerland's responsibility in denying shelter to threatened persons, a lucid look on the past cannot conceal the fact that Switzerland did welcome a significant number of Jews during the Nazi years. Nearly 29,000 Jews were granted asylum in Switzerland for varying periods of time. They accounted for about 10% of the number of persons admitted during this tragic era. Switzerland, a country with a population of about 4 million, welcomed a total of more than 300,000 persons on its territory if we add internees and deserters to the refugees. Moreover, we must point out that, during the war, in addition to the Jewish refugees, about 20,000 Jews were living in Switzerland; a little more than half of them were Swiss nationals and the others were foreign Jews living in Switzerland. None of them was threatened by the forces of National Socialism.

When comparing Switzerland's policy towards Jewish refugees with that of those other countries not subjected to the Axis powers, we observe that in its lack of generosity and openness Switzerland was in poor company, and that these countries were often far less generous in welcoming Jews whose life was threatened. Whereas Switzerland welcomed about 29,000 Jewish refugees, i.e. a little over 0.7% of its population, the United States accepted on its territory a mere 170,000 Jewish refugees, or 0.1% of its population – seven times less than Switzerland. Canada accepted 5,000 Jews only, i.e. fifteen times less than Switzerland in proportion to the respective populations of these countries. Great Britain welcomed about 50,000 Jews, or 0.1% of its population.

This tragic comparison does not excuse Switzerland but it gives an indication of what the general attitude was with regard to refugees in general and Jews in particular. As we have already noted above,[129] this attitude was apparent at the Evian Conference in 1938 and in the drastic measures taken by the Western countries (led by Great Britain and the United States) to limit the flow of refugees. It is also apparent in the fact that the Jewish Communities in many countries including Switzerland were required to accommodate the Jewish refugees.[130]

As to Switzerland, the fact the country was surrounded by the Axis forces and the necessity to prevent a German invasion may have helped to reinforce this restrictive policy toward Jewish refugees. The intention was to avoid irritating the Nazi leaders by welcoming too many Jews trying to escape their Nazi persecutors. Moreover, the Swiss Jews, fearing that this would affect their own situation, proved sometimes reluctant to welcome a high number of refugees. Jean-Jacques Langendorf writes: "For the Jews more than for other categories of refugees, the question was to know to what extent an admission policy could be applied without prompting a Nazi intervention. Moreover, as in other democracies, the Jewish establishment, particularly Saly Mayer from Saint-Gall, President of the Federation of Israelite Communities of Switzerland from 1936 to 1942, assisted by another person from Saint-Gall, Sidney Dreifuss, approached the head of the Police Division of the Federal Justice Department to ask him to restrain the admission of fellow Israelites to Switzerland. Of course, fear dictated such an approach: the fear of a massive arrival of 'Ostjuden', which would stir up Swiss anti-Semitism and discredit the 9,000 Swiss Israelites."[131]

Another factor that helped to restrict the acceptance of refugees in Switzerland is related to the particular situation of a

---

[129] Chapter 2.

[130] For precise data on Switzerland, see PICARD, J., *Die Schweiz und die Juden, 1933-1945*, Zurich, 1994.

[131] *"Le martyre de la neutralité"* (Neutrality as martyrdom) in *La Suisse face à l'Empire américain, op. cit.*, p. 90.

small country surrounded by the Axis powers, with little natural resources and fearing for its supplies in raw materials.

All this gives us a better explanation and understanding of what happened, but in no way does it justify the fact that more than 30,000 Jews were driven back, nor does it detract from the moral responsibility of those who decided and conducted this policy. Even though Switzerland, despite its difficult situation, welcomed a higher proportion of Jewish refugees than most other countries, it could and should have done more. In face of the tragic situation of the Jews who came to request asylum, it was impossible to claim that there was no more room. It has been difficult for Switzerland to acknowledge this fact and to draw all the conclusions from it for a long time, as shown by the very late rehabilitation of Paul Grüningen, a police officer heavily sanctioned for having organized the illegal entrance into Switzerland of several hundred Jews whose life he saved.

By refusing to open its doors more widely to Jewish refugees whose lives were directly threatened, Switzerland failed, at least in part, in the humanitarian duties of a neutral state. Daniel Thüre, a Swiss jurist, rightfully says that neutrals also have moral duties. "For instance, the duty to grant asylum to persecuted persons. Switzerland did not fully accept these humanitarian duties by sticking to a literal interpretation of the Code of neutrality."[132]

The requirements and the limits of a new reading of history

Switzerland is faced with – and is already resolutely committed to, particularly by establishing an international commission of historians presided by Jean-François Bergier – an ef-

[132] *Le Nouveau Quotidien*, August 21, 1997.

fort of memory which is not as easy to carry out as it seems at first sight. The persons who go through the exercise are required to be prepared to a sometimes-painful self-criticism. Moreover, the process is scattered with obstacles and has limits one should be aware of. First, it would be illusory and even dangerous to think that such a re-reading of history can generate truth through an accumulation of facts by researching archives. Historical facts as such do not generate truth: only interpretation gives them meaning. This is why it is difficult to give the label of truth to the results of the historian's work. In this respect, Jean-François Bergier, as a historian, prefers to speak of clarity rather than truth.[133] This role of interpretation becomes even essential in this Swiss effort of memory because we cannot expect many, important or entirely new facts to come out of the historians' work. All the facts related to this dark period have been known in their essentials for a long time. Historians will work on a reinterpretation and clarification of these facts.

This reinterpretation work can then be very dangerous if carried out only according to current criteria. It is true that each age has its own way of reinterpreting history according to its own values and requirements. Yet we cannot oppose any clarification of past actions by present values, for otherwise no moral progress would ever be possible and, for example, we could not condemn slavery. However, historical judgment is only possible if we consider the economic, social and political context of the past; otherwise we are leaving the field of history to work only in the political field or in that of ethics. Un-

---

[133] See in this respect *Neue Zürcher Zeitung*, January 22, 1997. See also the remarks made by a member of the commission, Jacques Picard: "Forschung zwischen politischem und wissenschatlichem Anspruch. Methodologische Grundlagen der Expertenkommission Bergier", *Neue Zürcher Zeitung*, October 28, 1997.

fortunately, such a bias is observed in the first Eizenstat report,[134] especially, as we have shown above, in the foreword written by Eizenstat himself. This trend is also observed in the Bergier interim report on transactions on gold operated by Switzerland,[135] as we have pointed out in this chapter. In many respects, and due to the a priori moral judgments made by its authors, this report relates more to ethics than to history. Even on this moral level, we feel that it does not take sufficient account of the economic and political circumstances of the period under review, which, according to the dichotomy established by Max Weber, pertains to an ethics of conviction as opposed to an ethics of responsibility. We could even speak of a counter-historical moralistic view that probably conceals deeply diverging views on the historical interpretation as such amongst the members of the Commission. Obviously, this report is the result of a hotly debated compromise. Because no true agreement could be reached on the historical analysis, there was a drift toward a moralistic view that projected the values of our times on the past, on which it was easier to agree.

Moreover, the possibility that the historians' reinterpretation work might become an instrument in the hands of political authorities should absolutely be avoided and yet, this is obviously what happened with the first Eizenstat report, due to the bias exhibited by Eizenstat's foreword, but also to the framework imposed on the historians who wrote the report. Willam M. Slany, who was responsible for this group of historians, acknowledged the fact when he declared, at an informative seminar held in Bern on June 20, 1997, that this unconventional historical research was dictated by the needs of the

[134] *U.S. and Allied Efforts to Recover and Restore Gold and other Assets Stolen or Hidden by Germany During World War II, op. cit.*

[135] *Switzerland and Gold Transactions in the Second World War, op. cit.*

policy-makers.[136] As to the Bergier Commission, we may wonder at length about its possible exploitation by the political authorities. In fact, they appointed the commission and the historians' work had to be done urgently to answer their requests. Antoine Maurice wrote that the creation of this commission "reflects a relationship with historical science which does not make the historians feel easy. On the one hand, when history is prepared in the workshops of a group of historians chosen by regal authority, it is made an instrument of political authorities. Endowed with a political power it does not demand, the Commission is instructed to produce punctually and in an almost journalistic way an official version, which somewhat recalls the practices of authoritarian regimes. On the other hand, serious disagreements on such a wide-ranging subject are likely to exist both at the input and output levels of the work of the commission."[137]

What was to be feared from the creation of such a commission was not that it should be led to exonerate Switzerland and its historical responsibilities, as Senator D'Amato and some leaders of the World Jewish Congress seemed to believe. On the contrary, what was to be feared was that the commission might be tempted, in view of the pressures on Switzerland, to give an interpretation to the history of Switzerland during World War II that would be too exclusively linked to current requirements and criteria, by dissociating the actions that were judged from their historical context. The commission might have become a judge making moral judgments. Unfortunately, as we have just shown, this is what apparently happened with the first interim report on gold. This justifies what Jean-Claude Favez, a historian, wrote soon after the commission was set up:

---

[136] *Journal de Genève*, June 21-22, 1997.

[137] *La Suisse face à l'Empire américain, op. cit.*, p. 9.

"Its goal it disputable and its results are constrained from the start. The commission will not be in a position to come out and say, 'we have found nothing.' Yet, when we undertake research work, we never know whether it will lead us somewhere. What did people want – a political commission? Then such a commission cannot claim that it will do scientific work. Yet this is the claim, although the work serves a political objective. This is what bothers me."[138]

There is a risk that, under external political pressures relayed by the Swiss political authorities, the official interpretation of Switzerland's wartime history, which gained acceptance soon after the war due to new events, in particular the emerging Cold War years, will be replaced by another politically contrived and therefore disputable interpretation.

Finally, this required effort of memory cannot be left to historians alone chosen by regal authority. The whole community of Swiss and foreign historians must undertake it. Even more so, it should be the effort of the Swiss people, for the historians' work would be useless if the Swiss themselves had no interest in the debate and were not ready to fully undertake an investigation of the dark and bright sides of their history, through a "process of reappropriation of the past"[139] with the same indefinite openness as history itself. In the words of Pierre Centlivres, an ethnologist, "to believe that historians alone can give a new meaning to historical facts which have been largely visited for fifty years is a mistake. It is not by churning out five tons of archives on what the Swiss did and said during the war – a necessary task indeed – that historians will find a totally different interpretation. The Swiss people as a whole must do the work, which cannot be delegated to a few special-

[138] *Ibid.*, p. 260.

[139] Yves Fricker in *La Suisse face à l'Empire américain, op. cit.*, p. 190.

ists to whom we would leave the uncomfortable facts and the embarrassing interpretations."[140] The collective work of the Swiss people is essential because this reappropriation of the past is a fundamental issue that requires, as we shall see in the next chapter, a new definition of the Swiss national identity.

[140] *Journal de Genève*, July 1, 1997.

Chapter six

The crisis, a catalyst for challenging national identity

Switzerland's effort of remembering and reassessing the past is obviously the consequence of external pressures stemming from the dormant assets and Nazi Gold crisis. Summoned to explain and to account for its past behavior by a number of Holocaust survivors and by Jewish organizations, relayed by some American politicians, Switzerland saw its international image challenged.

In the face of these external pressures, Switzerland was forced to react. After bitter negotiations, its major banks reached a global financial agreement with U.S. plaintiffs and the Jewish organizations after contributing, together with the Swiss National Bank, to a special Fund for immediate help to needy Holocaust survivors. As to the Swiss authorities, they adopted the legal provisions needed for a systematic investigation of dormant accounts, then they set up an independent international commission of historians to clarify all aspects of Switzerland's behavior during the darkest years of this century. We might feel that such answers to external pressures allowed Switzerland to end the crisis and that, apart from potential debates arising from future reports of the Commission of historians, it will gradually succeed in dispelling the bad image that was created, especially in the United States.

However, reducing this crisis to a mere challenging of an image developed outside of Switzerland would be a serious mistake. What lies at the heart of the crisis is not only the image of Switzerland that others may have, but first and foremost the image that the Swiss have of themselves. Over and above what Switzerland needs to account for with respect to others and to its own past lies the issue of national identity.

Challenging Swiss identity and its founding myths

Obviously, this crisis was widely echoed in Switzerland at the political level and in the media because external pressures and attacks directly impacted a country that is undergoing a difficult adaptation process to a deeply and rapidly evolving world and has to question the very foundations of its identity.[141] In that sense, we must acknowledge that the crisis was a catalyst of a process involving self-doubt and a self-questioning of Swiss national identity. This process started a few years ago with the deep changes in Switzerland's international environment. The image of Switzerland as a small, independent nation bravely defending democracy, law and justice, refusing to get involved in the conflicts between its neighbors while maintaining generosity, solidarity and an openness to the world, especially through its humanitarian commitments – this image was brought into doubt in a most violent way by a cer-

[141] See in this respect an excellent analysis by Yves Fricker: *Helvetia au miroir. Regards des autres et image de soi* (Switzerland in the mirror: self-image and the way others look at us) . Genève, Georg, 1996.

tain number of persons abroad. Such a criticism of Switzerland's behavior has greatly increased the need to challenge Swiss national identity. At the heart of this process the founding myths of this identity are brought into question.

Neutrality is a central element of this identity because it is rooted in a practice developed over the centuries. This practice has brought undeniable benefits to Switzerland. It has been at the core of a foreign and national security policy that allowed this country to avoid many devastating European conflicts. In an even more decisive way, neutrality has been an essential factor in maintaining national cohesion in a multicultural country, immersed in a highly conflictual European environment. Without neutrality, Switzerland would never have been in a position to survive as a state through past centuries.

In recent years, deep changes in Switzerland's international environment have challenged this neutrality. Two joint developments have undermined the foundations of Switzerland's policy of neutrality and, more generally, its national security policy: the cooperative and integrative process underway in Europe for the last forty years, and the major upheavals at the end of the '80s with the fall of the communist regimes, the end of the Cold War and the disappearance of the major blocs.

The first phenomenon has deeply changed the immediate environment of a country located right in the middle of Europe. For centuries, the environment had been of a highly conflictual nature and had culminated in two world wars in the 20th century. As this environment was threatening Switzerland's independence, internal cohesion and survival, the adoption of neutrality was fully justified. But through the development of the European community integration and, more generally, of a multidimensional cooperation in Western Europe, Switzerland, as the other European neutrals, became increasingly associated with a group of democratic countries that were not in conflict and were developing closer bonds of cooperation. This made new violence highly unlikely in the relationships between countries in this part of the Continent.

The transformation of Western Europe under the banner of cooperation and integration was unable, however positive it was, to challenge neutrality in its *raison d'être*. Europe was still separated in two blocs and an important conflict on the continent was still a serious threat. A policy of neutrality as a tool for national security remained relevant. In such a conflictual context, neutrals could offer their good offices to foster a form of peaceful coexistence between antagonistic blocs. We had to wait for the fall of the communist regimes in Europe and the end of the Cold War to have the right conditions for challenging neutrality radically. Once the threat of a war between the two major systems of alliances had vanished, the rationale for neutrality tended to lose ground. What could the benchmark for using neutrality? Moreover, challenging neutrality became increasingly unavoidable as European integration was gaining a new momentum. Neutral countries were compelled to find ways of participating directly in this communitarian integration for fear of being left out and acquiring a marginal status.

Challenging Swiss neutrality is no smooth process, however, because neutrality is so important in the Swiss national identity. Over time, the tool – and nothing but a tool - that neutrality should never have ceased to represent became an end in itself for many Swiss, an identity-related value that was essentially preserved to the point of becoming an object of worship. The political elite in power strengthened this mythical status of neutrality, notably since World War II, as it contributed greatly to national cohesion. Concealing what could be detrimental to this mythical vision fostered a certain image of neutrality. This is probably an all too common phenomenon, since any kind of power strives to foster and strengthen national cohesion by cultivating identity myths. To take only one example, this is what happened in liberated France when the image of French Resistance was projected.

Through the external pressures exerted on Switzerland, the crisis on dormant assets and Nazi Gold undoubtedly increased this questioning of neutrality. In particular, it showed how political authorities exploited neutrality as a mere instrument to conceal some aspects of Switzerland's behavior during World War II. In this sense, this crisis had beneficial consequences: it is not by staying locked in a dysfunctional myth that Switzerland will be in a position to meet the challenges of a world undergoing radical changes. However, owing to the abusive nature of the attacks against Switzerland and to the underlying political, economic and financial issues described in this book, Switzerland would be a loser if it let itself be drawn into a process of self-flagellation and did nothing more than replace one false interpretation of its history by a new, converse and equally disputable version.

In the face of these questions on the issue of neutrality since the close of the Cold War, strengthened today by the crisis over dormant assets and Nazi Gold, we need greater intellectual rigor to avoid the confusions and amalgamations that have been so frequently observed. The debate that has been taking place in Switzerland and in other neutral countries in Europe since the end of the Cold War is not related to the relevance and legitimacy of neutrality as it has been practiced in the past. The only problem is whether today, as Europe is liberated from the East-West conflict and is undergoing a process of integration, neutrality is still justified. With respect to whom and to avoid what conflict would neutrality be in Switzerland's interest? How could Switzerland's neighbors and, more generally, all European countries be interested in this neutrality?

What is central to the controversy raised by the crisis on dormant assets and Nazi Gold is neither the question of the adequacy of neutrality to the new challenges at the end of the 20th century, nor the question of its legitimacy as a political practice codified by international public law. What is at stake here is the way Switzerland used neutrality during World War II. More precisely, the problem is not whether Switzerland violated, through its behavior, the rules imposed on permanently neutral states by international public law. This would have been true if this country had embraced the Nazi cause, which obviously was not the case. The problem lies in the gap between the idealized and absolute image of neutrality Switzerland sought to convey, and actual Swiss behavior. In other words, this crisis raises questions because it reveals a discontinuity between the image of Swiss neutrality as a policy based on generosity, solidarity and humanitarian commitment, and some aspects of Switzerland's actual behavior during the dark years, in particular in its policy towards Jewish refugees. The legal aspects of neutrality are not at stake here, but its moral and political dimension – the myth of Switzerland using neutrality to serve a noble and humanitarian cause is put into doubt. What we see today is that the myth of neutrality as an absolute is debunked: we must relativize neutrality and consider it only as an instrument serving a national security policy, and not as an end in itself or a policy embodying moral integrity. Such a relativization of neutrality confirms the new assessment taking place in the light of the major changes occurring in Europe and in the international system at the end of this century.

The dangers of the Swiss exception

Ultimately, a form of Swiss exceptionalism underlies Switzerland's neutrality and humanitarian vocation, and it, too, also has to be challenged. For too long the Swiss have been convinced that their destiny was exceptional and that their privileged situation – no involvement in the violent conflicts which shattered Europe and, in the second part of this century, a prosperous economic situation – was due to their outstanding qualities as a people taking pride in its independence, a courageous, hard working, wise, peaceful people concerned by law and democracy and showing compassion for the misfortunes of the world. But today Europe is deeply transformed and, thanks to the process of integration, has achieved levels of stability, security and development comparable to Switzerland's own. In this respect, the Swiss are not an exception any longer in Europe but their situation is still somewhat exceptional in that they do not participate in the European integration process and in the United Nations Organization. They nevertheless gradually come to understand that this attitude only reinforces their isolation and might eventually threaten their well being and security.

The Swiss need to understand that the reason why they were violently attacked in this crisis and were in particular affected by the attacks does not lie in the fact that Switzerland's behavior was supposedly worse than that of other countries. While recognizing, as people begin to do now, the failings in Switzerland's past behavior, we must admit that, globally speaking and from a moral point of view, Switzerland behaved no worse than most of the other countries involved in World War II. If the Swiss are so vigorously attacked today, this is first of all because Swiss exceptionalism lies at the heart of their self-consciousness, and therefore of their identity. When we claim to be exceptional and of a superior moral essence, the fact that those that are judging us ask a lot from us should come as no surprise. We have today to admit that there is a hiatus between the image the Swiss constantly gave of themselves and some aspects of their behavior. This is true of our neutrality and, to an even greater extent, of Switzerland's humanitarian mission. This is also true of the highly specific image some people have sought to forge, sometimes very arrogantly, of the Swiss financial center . When confronted with troubled aspects of reality, such completely idealized images elicit only a sharp critical attitude in the way others look at us.

Today, Switzerland has to understand that it is just a country like any other. As for any country in the world, this should not imply that Switzerland should be deprived of its own peculiarities and distinctive features. This simply means that Switzerland is not of a higher moral essence.

Interestingly enough, Swiss exceptionalism shares some common features with American exceptionalism. Even if Switzerland never adopted the typically messianic American attitude, the two nations share a strong belief in an exceptional destiny, in a defense of values embedding a superior moral essence. It might be rightfully objected that each people has elements of exceptionalism in its identity and consciously develops its own genius. In the case of Switzerland and the United States, however, this feeling is particularly strong and determines specific behaviors. Whereas the United States tends to project its moral superiority universally according to its interests as a superpower, Switzerland is far from having such a messianic attitude but seeks to hide behind its own values and exceptionalism as a protection against the turmoil of the world.

Toward openness and solidarity

A new reading of the past alone is not enough to bring a direct answer to the problems of today. By forcing the Swiss to make a critical reappraisal of their founding myths, by serving as a catalyst of an identity crisis that has been latent for a number of years, it will nevertheless help them to redefine their place and their role in the world today and to adapt better to a rapidly evolving environment. This process is not easy and holds no guarantees for the future. We might fear that, in the wake of the violent and immoderate attacks against their country during the crisis, the Swiss could be tempted to retreat back into a defensive and melancholic attitude. This would unfortunately only add to the current difficulties they have in adapting to a changing world. This is the reason why Switzerland, while taking a hard look at its detractors' motives and the abuse hurled at it, must take advantage of the shock created by this crisis to think over again the foundations of its identity and try to redefine itself with respect to its environment.

In our opinion, the one and only possible answer to Switzerland's problems, including the questions raised by the crisis on dormant assets and Nazi Gold, lies in openness and solidarity. The smear campaign against Switzerland during this crisis showed how vulnerable an isolated country can be. This growing isolation in the new European and international context is a deep source of concern for the future of this country. As fully recognized by the Swiss government, the fact that Switzerland is not a member of major decision-making authorities such as the European Union and United Nations Organization can only weaken its position on the international scene and worsen its vulnerability. This isolation restricts Switzerland's possible contribution to peace and stability in

Europe, for it would be illusory to believe that the good offices of a neutral country are still really useful nowadays. If Switzerland is to contribute to peace and stability in Europe and in the world, it is not through the exceptionalism of a mythified neutrality, but through a full involvement in the institutions set up to meet the challenges of the world today. Switzerland must abandon its solitary journey to become resolutely committed to European construction and the United Nations. True, these institutions have their problems and participation will imply costs or even a certain amount of risk. Such costs and risks are lower, however, than those that isolation would necessarily mean. The Swiss must understand that it is not possible for them any more to be present in world affairs without being actually committed and assuming the costs and the risks.

The resolute choice of openness with respect to others and of involvement in world affairs will allow Switzerland to recover its lost sense of solidarity. Instead of freezing solidarity into a myth, we must live it by sharing our own world with others and assuming all the risks involved. In this respect, the project of a Swiss Foundation for Solidarity launched by the Swiss government when this crisis was reaching its climax should be given full support, provided that it operates in the wider perspective of openness to the world. Otherwise it might be but an ersatz of true solidarity, a way of indulging in self-satisfaction and good conscience.

Epilogue

Switzerland, the first stage in a global strategy

Switzerland's painful experience with the Jewish dormant assets and Nazi Gold issues have abundantly proven the snowball nature of the crisis. Other countries are and will be affected too.

First of all, as we have observed, beyond its singularity this violent crisis is part of the reassessing of the past of all European countries and other World War II protagonists.

But in the months following the global agreement reached on August 12, 1998, there occurred a series of events (involving the major Swiss banks, the World Jewish Congress and the initiators of the U.S. class actions suits) showing that Switzerland was only the first link in a chain – and the first to break. Thus, building on this first success, the World Jewish Congress and a group of class action plaintiffs turned their attacks on other countries – notably France, Germany and Austria – and several big American companies.

For example, a class action suit was filed against several French banks in the U.S. The banks stand accused of having made money from dormant accounts, negligently restituted the accounts after World War II, and of keeping no record of

Holocaust victims' accounts. As for the wartime spoliation suffered by French Jews, the World Jewish Congress on several occasions eagerly asked for the results of the work of the Mattéoli Mission, a task force set up by the French government in February 1997. The Mattéoli Mission's final report on the spoliation of French Jews was expected towards the end of 1999 only, but the World Jewish Congress has already declared it is determined to obtain quick restitution and compensation. The World Jewish Congress also asked that 2,000 art works stolen from Jews, now in French museums, be sold and the proceeds given to Jewish charities. At least the French authorities, supported by French Jews, have so far succeeded in avoiding any direct interference of American Jewish organizations, notably the World Jewish Congress.

In the United States class action suits were filed against Ford and General Motors. These companies' German subsidiaries are accused of having supported the Nazi war effort and of using forced labor.

In Germany and in Austria too U.S. class action suits were filed against several banks and companies, there involving forced labor in German companies. In January 1999, the World Jewish Congress announced that it would oppose any merger between Deutsche Bank and Bankers Trust, an American bank, if the German bank did not offer compensation to Holocaust victims, adding that it was prepared to start an international boycott campaign similar to the campaign against Swiss banks if Deutsche Bank refused to comply. It also called for a quick global financial settlement involving not only Deutsche Bank but also other German companies concerned by the forced labor issue.

To date Germany (i.e. German government, banks, companies) had already paid compensation amounting to more than 100 billion marks to Nazi victims. Learning the lessons from the Swiss experience, Germany was quick to bow to the pressure and threats of the Jewish organizations and class action initiators and engage in negotiations in the U.S. (under the auspices of Under Secretary of State Stuart Eizenstat). On December 14th 1999, an agreement was reached between the lawyers for the estimated 2.3 million surviving victims of Third Reich's forced labor program and the German industry and government. The agreement will have 255 companies and the German government pay DM 10 billion ($5.2 billion) into a compensation fund.

All this goes to show that the Swiss crisis was obviously part of a wider strategy now being applied to other countries. This strategy is very efficient over the short term. But the methods used are morally flawed. They focus on financial aspects, thereby doing a disservice to the just and noble cause of Jews around the world. The remembrance of the Holocaust should have taken precedence. Instead, it has been flouted.